THE PSYCHOLOGIST-MANAGER JOURNAL

Volume 8, Number 2, 2005

THE PSYCHOLOGIST-MANAGER JOURNAL

Subscriber Information

Subscriptions: *The Psychologist-Manager Journal* is published two times a year by Lawrence Erlbaum Associates, Inc., 10 Industrial Avenue, Mahwah, NJ 07430–2262. Subscriptions for Volume 8, 2005, are available only on a calendar-year basis. Individual rates: **Print *plus* online:** $75.00 in US/Canada, $105.00 outside US/Canada. Institutional rates: **Print-only:** $235.00 in US/Canada, $265.00 outside US/Canada. **Online-only:** $225.00 in US/Canada and outside US/Canada. **Print *plus* online:** $250.00 in US/Canada, $280.00 outside US/Canada. Visit LEA's Web site at http://www.erlbaum.com to view a free sample. Send subscription orders to the Journal Subscription Department, Lawrence Erlbaum Associates, Inc., 10 Industrial Avenue, Mahwah, NJ 07430–2262; e-mail: journals@erlbaum.com

Change of address: Address changes should include the mailing label or facsimile. Send address changes to the Journal Subscription Department, Lawrence Erlbaum Associates, Inc., 10 Industrial Avenue, Mahwah, NJ 07430–2262.

Claims: Claims for missing issues cannot be honored beyond 4 months after the mailing date. Duplicate copies cannot be sent to replace issues not delivered due to failure to notify publisher of change of address.

This journal is abstracted or indexed in EBSCOhost Products and PsychInfo.

THE PSYCHOLOGIST-MANAGER JOURNAL, 2005, 8(2), 103–104

Introduction to Special Issue: Legal and Forensic Issues in Management

Jay M. Finkelman

California School of Business and Organizational Studies
Alliant International University

I am delighted to have assembled an august group of lawyers and psychologists to highlight some of the fascinating legal and forensic issues that have now become part of the management process. When Peter Drucker first established management as a true professional activity, there was not a lot of technical information available to facilitate the process. But management is not only about lofty concepts and ideas, it is also about risk management and how to avoid lawsuits and costly litigation.

Over the years the availability of increasingly more sophisticated strategies and tactics inexorably changed the role of management. This special issue focuses in detail on precisely those strategies and tactics that relate to the challenges of risk management and employment law. The reader will gain insight as to what general managers should be aware of and the specifics that risk managers need attend to. The psychologist–manager is in a unique position to benefit from this counsel and to develop remedies, as appropriate.

The strategies and tactics described by the authors are excellent ways to avoid litigation, although they certainly do not purport to substitute for professional legal advice specific to your organization. Though much of the analysis is from the perspective of a corporate defendant, a plaintiff's attorney also provides insight as to how Human Resource Management testimony is used to support allegations of discrimination, harassment, and retaliation.

Mort McPhail presents a sophisticated risk assessment model to "audit" the liability associated with the personnel selection process. Katy Fodchuk and Eric Sidebotham, Esq., present recent research and litigation relating to applicants' per-

Correspondence should be sent to Jay M. Finkelman, California School of Business and Organizational Studies, Alliant International University, 1000 S. Fremont Avenue, Unit 5, Alhambra, CA 91803. E-mail: jfinkelman@alliant.edu

ceptions of fairness for selection procedures. In addition, suggestions for employers concerning methods for incorporating fairness in the selection process are offered.

Clement Glynn, Esq., and Quin Marshall, Esq., provide a prophylactic approach to reduce the level of risk typically leading to employment litigation. Eric Sidebotham, Esq., discusses the appropriate and necessary use of documentation to reduce the probability and severity of litigation. Donna Rutter, Esq., offers a detailed analysis of the best way to manage the awkward situation of a employing a plaintiff who is litigating against your organization.

Lawrence J. Song, Esq., and Jonathan M. Turner, Esq., present an intriguing overview of the effect of employment laws on the increasingly popular practice of employee leasing. Gene Vorobyov, Esq., considers the legal implications of the ubiquitous use of computers and the internet in the workplace, from a refreshingly common sense perspective. Tom Dinkelacker, Esq., describes the consequences of having workers distracted by the use of cell phones while driving in your employ.

Jan Nielsen, Esq., documents the evolution of human resource management testimony in employment litigation, and addresses a recent appellate court decision in California. Rodney Lowman integrates the various perspectives and approaches encompassed in this special issue within a fascinating discussion of the newly developing roles for psychologists in industry as managers and as professionals.

The world of business and management has changed dramatically since the early insightful observations and analysis of Peter Drucker. The role of the psychologist–manager has expanded significantly and human resource managers have gained increasing credibility and responsibility. Risk management has taken on a heightened level of strategic importance and has become a key component in the profitability of many organizations.

This special issue of *TPMJ* presents an array of legal and forensic challenges, analyses, and solutions that should prove interesting and useful for psychologist–managers, all levels of management and students of management.

ACKNOWLEDGMENTS

As Special Issue Editor, I gratefully acknowledge the contribution and the assistance of Peng Fu, a doctoral student in the California School of Business and Organizational Studies at Alliant International University, in the organization and assembly of the manuscripts.

THE PSYCHOLOGIST-MANAGER JOURNAL, 2005, *8*(2), 105–120

Ψ I. MANAGEMENT PRINCIPLES: THE THEORY OF MANAGEMENT

Procedural Justice in the Selection Process: A Review of Research and Suggestions for Practical Applications

Katy Mohler Fodchuk
Old Dominion University

Eric J. Sidebotham
Attorney-at-Law

A job applicant's perception of whether a selection process is fair constitutes an important factor for employers to take into consideration when designing hiring and promotional selection procedures. It is evident that the outcome of a selection process has a potentially profound impact on a job applicant (e.g., hiring, rejection, promotion). If that selection outcome is negative and the process is perceived as unfair by the applicant, some aspect of the process, or the process in its entirety, may become the basis for a discrimination lawsuit against the employer. This article presents the concept of procedural justice and considers factors influencing whether a procedure is perceived as fair as well as recent research concerning an instrument for assessing procedural justice as it relates to the selection process. In addition, a real world example of a legal "job-relatedness" challenge to a selection process (one aspect of procedural justice) is discussed. Finally, useful ideas concerning methods for incorporating procedural justice in the selection process are offered.

Greenberg and Lind (2000), prominent researchers in the field of organizational justice, have reviewed a compilation of the justice literature and discussed the application of this research in field settings. Since their review, new research (Bauer et al., 2001; Truxillo, Bauer, Paronto, & Campion, 2002) has identified tools avail-

Correspondence should be addressed to Katy Mohler Fodchuk, Department of Psychology, Organizational Research Group, MGB 250, Old Dominion University, Norfolk, VA 23503. E-mail: kfodchuk@odu.edu

able to practitioners to develop new or redesign existing selection processes that will be perceived as fair by job applicants. The selection process is an important employment practice upon which to focus because its results can have a profound impact on a job applicant (e.g., hiring, rejection, promotion) and may act as the basis for a discrimination lawsuit against the employer.

PROCEDURAL JUSTICE

Greenberg and Lind (2000) defined the overall structure of organizational justice in terms of principles deriving from the prevailing ideologies of distributive justice, "the fairness of the way outcomes are distributed," and procedural justice, "the fairness of the procedures used to determine those distributions" (p. 77). Positive outcomes in the organizational setting can include distribution of resources such as money (e.g., raises or bonuses), job offers, benefits, and promotions. Negative outcomes can include rejection of an applicant, demotion, disciplinary actions, and pay reduction.

Distributive justice is tied to Adams' (1965) equity principle, which stated that to produce a sense of equity, what employees obtain from an organization should be proportional to their relative contributions. Greenberg and Lind (2000) stated that when forming a judgment, what is *perceived* as fair is often more important than what *is* actually fair. In reference to equity theory, Greenberg and Lind stated that problems arise in situations "in which 'inputs' are not clearly defined ... [as] people will tend to distort their own contributions upward, relative to others" (p. 78).

Leventhal (1980) was the first to identify procedural rules or rules used informally to determine whether a procedure is fair. Leventhal proposed that the context of the situation (e.g., selection exam, performance evaluation, etc.) would dictate which procedural rule should be employed. Further, Leventhal defined the influence of a rule on an individual's judgment of procedural fairness as a weight. The greater the expectation one has for the rule's application, the greater its weight. Thus, in a given context, when an expected procedural rule was not applied, procedural justice would be violated. The procedural rules proposed by Leventhal included consistency (allocation procedures should be consistently applied to all persons across time), bias suppression (procedures are free of personal self-interest and narrow views), accuracy (decisions are based on as much good information and informed opinion as possible), correctability (decisions can be modified or reversed if needed), representativeness (basic concerns, values, and outlook of all parties are taken into account), and ethicality (existing ethical and moral principles are followed). In addition to Leventhal's six procedural rules, Thibaut and Walker (1975) identified process control or voice (i.e., procedure allows for expression of opinions and dialog from all concerned parties) and Bies and Moag (1986) identified interactional justice, which is comprised of social sensitivity (i.e., parties treat one another with respect and dignity) and justification by information (i.e., information concerning the procedure is given to those affected by its outcome).

REVIEW OF RESEARCH SURROUNDING PROCEDURAL JUSTICE AND SELECTION

Research has explored applicant perceptions of procedural justice and the selection process, including an assessment of the fairness reactions for different types of selection techniques used by employers (Smither, Reilly, Millsap, Pearlman, & Stoffey, 1993; Steiner & Gilliland, 1996), analysis of the effects of procedural and distributive justice on reactions to selection systems (Gilliland, 1994), and a comparison of the reactions of two applicant pools where procedural justice rules were implemented for one (Truxillo et al., 2002).

According to Greenberg and Lind (2000), industrial/organizational (I/O) psychologists often view fairness in the selection process as denoting procedures that have sound psychometric properties (e.g., job-relatedness, validity, and reliability). In a survey of French and American college students, Steiner and Gilliland (1996) found that both samples (also previous job applicants) rated work-sample tests, interviews, and resumes with the highest favorability out of a number of selection measures. However, selection techniques that are favored by applicants may be lacking content or construct validity. For example, although work-sample tests and a well-structured interview have a consistently high validity (Schmidt & Hunter, 1998), resumes are most likely not used in a manner that is methodical enough to determine validity.

It is not wise to completely customize the selection process to the preferences of applicants, due to psychometric considerations and legal guidelines. In certain circumstances, deviations from prior practices or official policies of the employer could cause one to run afoul of antidiscrimination laws. However, as Smither et al. (1993) point out, applicant reactions to a selection process should at least be of practical concern to process developers for three reasons: organizational attractiveness (e.g., applicant's intent to accept job offer, recommendation for others to apply at organization), applicant reactions and the likelihood of litigation, and reactions affecting both validity and utility of the selection process.

Smither et al. (1993) found that applicants' reactions to selection examinations were positively related to procedural and distributive justice perceptions, organizational attractiveness, and willingness to recommend the employer to others. In addition, Gilliland (1994) found employees who believed their employer used fair selection procedures expressed more positive attitudes toward their work and displayed higher performance than those who believed their employer used unfair practices. Finally, Singer (1992, 1993) found that job applicants were less likely to accept offers if they viewed the selection procedure as unfair. These studies support the reasons for implementing procedural justice in selection.

It is important to note that research has found that some valid practices (i.e., from an I/O psychologist's perspective) are perceived as fair by applicants. Specifically, applicant procedural justice ratings were higher for selection practices that were perceived as job-related and possessing predictive validity (Ployhart & Ryan, 1997; Smither et al. 1993; Steiner & Gilliland, 1996; Truxillo et al., 2002) and process favorability ratings were higher for procedures having a strong scientific basis (for Americans sampled in Steiner & Gilliland, 1996).

NEW RESOURCES FOR ASSESSING PROCEDURAL JUSTICE PERCEPTIONS OF APPLICANTS

A key question raised by this discussion is how one finds out whether the selection procedures currently used in one's organization are perceived as fair by applicants. Fortunately, Bauer et al. (2001) have developed a comprehensive scale assessing applicant reactions to selection procedures. This scale incorporated procedural justice rules that relate specifically to the selection process.

This assessment tool was termed the Selection Procedural Justice Scale (SPJS), and can be used to identify whether specific procedural justice rules are being incorporated in the selection process, from the perspective of applicants.To orient the reader to the theoretical foundation upon which the SPJS was based, it is important first to present Gilliland's (1993) theoretical and empirically supported model of procedural justice rules that specifically apply to the selection context. Ten procedural justice rules were proposed, based on the organizational justice literature and applicant reaction models, and two additional possible rules were presented based on more limited research. Gilliland organized the ten procedural rules into three categories: formal characteristics, explanation, and interpersonal treatment.

Gilliland's procedural justice rules related to selection.   Procedural rules in the formal characteristics (of the selection process) subgroup included: job relatedness, opportunity to perform, reconsideration opportunity, and consistency of administration. Job relatedness concerns the degree to which a test seems to assess content that is relevant to the job or that appears valid (Gilliland, 1993). Job relatedness ties back to Leventhal's (1980) accuracy rule and Sheppard and Lewicki's (1987) evidence for a resource rule which proposes that decisions need to be supported by accurate resources and expertise. Gilliland proposed that the opportunity to perform rule was based to the voice rule (Thibaut & Walker, 1975) and, in the context of selection, an applicant's voice can be construed as having sufficient opportunity to demonstrate one's knowledge, skills, and abilities in the testing setting

(Arvey & Sackett, 1993). Reconsideration opportunity entails the extent to which an applicant is able to contest or change the evaluation process and relates to Leventhal's (1980) correctibility rule and Greenberg's findings concerning the ability to challenge a decision (1986). Finally, the consistency of administration rule draws on research and theory surrounding the standardization of decision making procedures (Leventhal, 1980; Tyler & Bies, 1990). In relation to the testing situation, Arvey and Sackett (1993) proposed that consistency refers to the selection system's content, scoring procedures, and score interpretation. Leventhal (1980) suggested that consistency had distributive underpinnings, detailing that individuals should have an equal opportunity to receive the decision outcome or, in this case, appointment to the desired position.

Procedural rules detailed in the explanation category included feedback, selection information, and honesty. These rules correspond to factors identified in the interactional justice literature (Tyler & Bies, 1990). The feedback rule entails the extent to which an applicant receives timely and informative feedback concerning his or her test performance (Gilliland, 1993). Selection information concerns whether justification for a decision is provided to the applicant and is likely related to the validity of the selection process and information concerning the weight of a selection measure's results in the decision making process. The honesty rule concerns the extent to which interactions between applicant and the organization representative (e.g., interviewer, test administrator) are perceived as honest and truthful from the perspective of the applicant. Gilliland (1993) notes that honesty may be inherent in the rules of selection information and feedback but points to research (i.e., Liden & Parsons, 1986; Schmitt & Coyle, 1976) that suggests honesty is a distinct construct influencing applicant reactions.

The interpersonal treatment subgroup included the interpersonal effectiveness of the administrator, two-way communication, and propriety of questions rules. Interpersonal effectiveness of the administrator refers to the extent to which the applicant perceives the test administrator as thoughtful, respectful, and warm (Gilliland, 1993). Two-way communication, which can also be traced back to Thibaut and Walker's (1975) voice rule, concerns the degree to which applicants have the ability to participate and have their position and opinions considered in the selection process. In a selection situation two-way communication can refer to an applicant's ability to ask questions regarding the job, the organization, or the selection process (Gilliland, 1993). Research from Bies and Moag (1986) suggested that the propriety of questions asked in the selection process factors into applicant fairness perceptions. Specifically, questions that are both improper and biased, termed by Leventhal (1980) as violating the *bias suppression rule*, were found to influence procedural justice perceptions in recruits (Bies & Moag, 1986).

Gilliland (1993) also suggested two other possible procedural rules that were not as well researched and did not have ties to organizational justice theory and research. These rules included the ease of faking answers and invasiveness of questions or invasion of privacy. The ease of faking rule concerns whether an applicant believes that the information he or she provides during the selection process can easily be altered to appear more desirable to the organization (e.g., an applicant may have a hard time deciding whether to be honest or lie to appear as a better candidate). Gilliland (1993) referenced a review (Stone & Stone, 1990) of the types of factors that contribute to an applicant's perception of privacy invasion. Specifically, the type of test and the manner in which it is implemented can have an impact on perceived invasion of privacy. Gilliland discussed the need for more research for these final two rules to link them to perceived fairness and procedural justice.

Development of the Selection Procedural Justice Scale.

As stated previously, the SPJS can be used to identify whether specific procedural justice rules are being incorporated in the selection process, from the perspective of applicants. Bauer et al. (2001) conducted an extensive 5-phase study to develop the scale including the generation and refinement of items: an exploratory factor analysis using actual job applicants, confirmation of the factors with a separate group of applicants, an analysis of convergent and divergent validity, and finally a test of the generalizability of the remaining items using student samples. The reader is referred to Bauer et al. for a complete listing of the scale items.

The SPJS contains Structure higher-order factor and Social higher-order factor subscales as well as a third Job-relatedness–Content factor. The Structure higher-order factor subscales address process or procedure which can be manipulated by changing the actual structure of the selection process, including the information provided, chance to perform, feedback or reconsideration opportunities, or predictive job relatedness. For example, if it is found that applicant reactions reveal low ratings for the "Information Known" items, the selection process developers can revise job announcements, application packets, or instructions given during the selection process to include more information on the actual selection process itself. This portion of the scale is similar to Gilliland's (1993) formal characteristics category as it entails rules associated with specific properties of the selection process.

The Social higher-order factor subscales are related to interactional justice principles, first identified by Bies and Moag (1986), in that these items assess the applicant's perception of how he or she is treated on an interpersonal level: communication, openness, treatment, respect, consistency, and propriety. Although communication is definitely involved in the Structure higher-order factor subscales, the Social higher-order factor set of scales deals more with the manner in which the assessment was administered than the actual structure of procedure itself. For example, great pains can be taken to ensure the structure of the selection exam is psychometrically sound; however, if the person administering this selection exam treats certain applicants adversely based on his or her biases toward certain groups, all the effort expended during the development of the sound selection exam can be lost.

Finally, the Job-relatedness–Content items did not load on the Social or Structure factors but were retained as a separate factor. Applicant reactions on this scale could alert employers to whether applicants believe the content of the selection exam appears to be related to the job to which the applicant is applying. Bauer and colleagues (2001) speculate that different selection procedures are most likely "not perceived simply as 'fair' or 'unfair' by applicants, but rather as fair in some ways but not in others" (p. 414). The key strength of the SPJS is that it allows users to delineate precisely what aspect(s) of their selection process are perceived as unfair.

Of interest, the predictive job-relatedness and job-relatedness content issues are heavily scrutinized in an adverse impact claim under the Civil Rights Act of 1964, known generally as Title VII. Although the SPJS was not used by the employer in the following lawsuit, it is offered as a real-world example of what can occur when applicants perceive that the job-relatedness rule has been violated. Instances where the SPJS may have shed some light on negative applicant reactions that resulted in the lawsuit will be highlighted and discussed. This lawsuit also illustrates how the courts interpret and implement procedural justice rules in the area of selection criteria.

A CASE EXAMPLE OF PROCEDURAL JUSTICE ISSUES UNDERLYING A DISCRIMINATION COMPLAINT

A significant case illustrates the issues that exist in the selection process which could be addressed by the SPJS, in particular the job-relatedness–predictive criterion. In *Association of Mexican-American Educators v. State of California,* 213 F.3d 572 (9th Cir. 2000), the California Basic Education Skills Test (CBEST) was challenged on a theory of disparate impact. The CBEST purports to assess and verify the acceptable proficiency in reading, writing, and mathematics skills in the English language for California teachers. In most circumstances, before a person can be credentialed to teach K–12 in California, that person must first take and pass the CBEST.

As a backdrop, it was alleged that there was a shortage of teachers in California when the case was filed. The shortage was claimed to be the worst in areas under economic pressure, such as inner cities. The plaintiffs were racial minorities who took and failed the CBEST. The trial court found that the CBEST had an adverse impact on the plaintiff class but also found that the defendants successfully showed that the CBEST was a "valid, job-related test for the teaching and nonteaching positions in public schools for which it is a requirement" (213 F.3d at 587, 2000).

The case focused on whether the CBEST was properly validated. Where there is a scored test, such as the CBEST, the Ninth Circuit requires a showing that the test is job-related, such that it actually measures skills, knowledge, or ability required for the successful performance of the job. According to the Court, the employer must first specify the particular trait or characteristic which the selection device is being used to identify or measure. Next, the employer must determine that the particular trait or characteristic is an important element of work behavior. Finally, the employer must show, by professionally acceptable methods, that the selection device is predictive of or significantly correlated with the element of work behavior identified in the second step.

In terms of procedural justice, allegations did not concern the issues tapped by the Social higher-order factor subscales. The problem centered on the question of job-relatedness, specifically, whether the CBEST contained items that tested the requisite knowledge, skills, and abilities required for teachers in the state of California. The plaintiff class felt that perhaps they were not given a chance to perform. For example, many of the class members had skills that were not assessed by the CBEST but that they argued were job-related. Specifically, there was a question about language skills in schools in which a language other than English is the norm, which is not part of the CBEST. Indeed, part of the reason the plaintiffs brought the lawsuit is likely due to deficiencies that could have been identified by the Structure higher-order factor subscales.

Three validity studies were presented by the defendants at the trial court (Association of Mexican-American Educators v. State of California, 1996). The first two, which the court characterized as content validation studies, comprised the use of teachers to rate the CBEST test questions for relevancy to the job. In the first two studies a subject matter expert group composed of teachers rated the CBEST test questions for relevancy to the job. The third study, performed by Dr. Kathleen Lundquist in 1994 and 1995, consisted of a job analysis survey and content validation study.

The survey involved several steps. First, a literature search was conducted on the basic skill requirement for teaching at the kindergarten through 12th grade levels. Then 52 teachers from various grade levels, geographic locations, and ethnic groups were interviewed regarding their job activities, their use of reading, writing, and mathematics and other knowledge, skills, and abilities used on the job. Eighteen were also observed on the job. All the information gathered was then used to draft a preliminary list of skills and activities used by teachers.

After the information was gathered, panels of content experts reviewed the list of skills and abilities. The panels also evaluated the skills required to use actual curricular materials. The panels then linked the skill requirements to the job activities. Most of the skills were determined to be required for using the curricular materials *and* for performing activities on the job. Lundquist concluded that there was a strong linkage of skills to activities. The court, however, did not discuss whether knowledge statements were incorporated in the analysis.

Finally, the job analysis survey was created based on all of the collected materials. The California Commission on Teacher Credentialing (CTC) reviewed the survey which was then pilot tested. Afterward, the final survey was broadly distributed. Lundquist employed a high standard to identify important activities and skills. Certain anomalies resulted from the survey mostly in the mathematics section, which surprised even the CTC. Indeed, the CTC commissioned Lundquist to perform another content validity study to reexamine the math skills on the CBEST. That further content validity study resulted in modifications of the CBEST. The trial court responded to criticisms of the plaintiffs by stating that "the decision to reexamine the math skills and the process by which Dr. Lundquist conducted the content validity study reflect sound professional judgments in light of the questionable results of the job analysis survey" (937 F. Supp. 1397, 1996).

In the end, the Ninth Circuit found the three validation studies to be acceptable for defendants to rebut the statistical disparate impact *prima facie* case established by the plaintiff class. The Court, in a sharply divided opinion, recognized that "[v]alidation studies are, by their very nature difficult, expensive, time consuming and rarely, if ever, free of error" (213 F.3d at 587, 2000).

The dissent, led by Judge Stephen Reinhardt, criticized the majority's opinion on the ground that the validation studies failed to differentiate between different school jobs, and that the test items of the CBEST were predictive of or significantly correlated to job related skills through a study the trial court found to be "unscientific" and "not particularly helpful" (213 F.3d at 594, 2000). In particular, Judge Reinhardt criticized what may be the central weakness of the CBEST from a procedural justice perspective—its failure to include language specialization in geographic locations where English may not be the primary language. The trial court quoted *Connecticut v. Teal,* 457 U.S. 440 (1982) for the proposition that the CBEST is nothing more than a "testing mechanism with a built-in headwind for minority groups" (937 F. Supp. 1408, 1996). Reinhardt's dissent from the Ninth Circuit opinions was echo of the *Connecticut v. Teal* sentiments of the trial court, where the United States Supreme Court expressly said, "Congress' primary purpose [for enacting Title VII] was the prophylactic one of achieving equality in employment opportunities and removing barriers to such equality" (457 U.S. at 448–449). Judge Reinhardt also tacitly acknowledged that there was a severe teacher shortage in California and that qualified minority candidates could have filled some of those positions except for the CBEST.

IDEAS FOR IMPLEMENTING PROCEDURAL
JUSTICE IN THE SELECTION PROCESS

Research in the field of selection has presented some very compelling reasons to investigate whether selection practices are perceived as fair and to attempt to improve practices where procedural justice perceptions are low. Information on applicant reactions provided by the SPJS could be valuable to employers if they actually used it to implement real change in their selection process. The case involving the CBEST challenge offers a good example. For example, allegations in this case concerned the issues tapped by the Social higher-order factor subscales. The legal challenge focused on the question of job-relatedness of the CBEST and whether the plaintiffs were provided the opportunity to perform. In particular, many of the class members had skills (i.e., language skills) that were not assessed by the CBEST but that they argued were job-related. It is important now to discuss methods for implementing changes in the selection process that could potentially minimize the risk of such a lawsuit.

Structure Higher-Order Scales

Much of the research in this area establishes the link between procedural justice perceptions and specific outcomes and some of this research goes further to outline specific and practical recommendations for employers to improve their existing selection methods with regard to procedural justice perceptions (Gilliland, 1994; Lounsbury, Borbrow, & Jenson, 1989; Smither et al., 1993; Truxillo et al., 2002). Consider the procedural justice rules of job relatedness–content and job-relatedness–predictive, operationalized from Gilliland (1993) by Bauer et al. (2001). Smither et al. (1993) measured perceived predictive and face validity of different selection measures and found that entry-level managers and recruitment and employment managers judged simulations, interviews, and cognitive tests with relatively concrete item-types to be significantly more job-related than personality, biodata, and cognitive tests with relatively abstract item-types. In addition, Lounsbury et al. (1989) found that subjects display more favorable attitudes concerning testing when told about the relation between the test and future job performance.

Although it appears that research has not yet analyzed a link between job-relatedness perceptions and Gilliland's (1993) procedural justice rule of opportunity to perform, it seems plausible that applicants who perceived the content of the selection measure to be job-related would be more likely to perceive that they were allowed to show their job skills and abilities through the test than those who did not perceive the selection measure as job-related. As mentioned previously, the plaintiffs in *Association of Mexican-American Educators v. State of California* (2000) claimed they did not have an adequate chance to perform. These plaintiffs felt that their specialized language skills were job-related and, because they were not measured or taken into account by the CBEST, largely ignored.

One possible recommendation for implementing the opportunity to perform would be to include more than one job-related measure of performance in instances where the job calls for assessment of a variety of skill sets. For example, an employment consultant position might require knowledge of relevant employment laws and guidelines as well as analytical skills used during job analysis and the development of employment selection examinations. In addition, this position might entail a large amount of client contact, facilitation of meetings, and group presenta-tions. If the selection process were composed only of a cognitive written exam as-sessing analytical skills and knowledge of employment law, those candidates with a high level of interpersonal communication and presentation skills might feel that they did not have the chance to perform and that the selection process was biased.

Research surrounding Gilliland's (1993) procedural justice rules of selection information and feedback has shown that relatively inexpensive means can help in-crease applicant procedural justice perception ratings. Information provided in the form of a job announcement or informational flyer can address applicant questions at key stages of the selection process or even before it begins. In a study examining the relationship between the amount of information applicants received concern-ing the selection process and procedural justice perceptions, it was found that ap-plicants who received more information had significantly higher perceptions of procedural justice (Truxillo et al., 2002). This information included a brief de-scription of how a selection measure was developed (covering job-relatedness rule) and how long it would take to score the measure (covering the feedback rule).

When attempting to implement the reconsideration opportunity rule (Gilliland, 1993), employers can schedule a specific time for applicants to review the results of their selection exam or measure with the administrator or selection process de-veloper. Applicants should also be made aware that this opportunity exists (e.g., through job announcement or informational flyer, during the instruction readings for a selection examination). The selection staff conducting the review should have a thorough knowledge of the specific testing process to answer appropriately any of the applicant's questions concerning his or her performance. Table 1 outlines each of the aforementioned Structure higher-order factor subscales and offers rec-ommendations for implementing procedural justice into the selection process.

Social Higher-Order Factor Scales

As mentioned previously the Social higher-order factor subscales (i.e., consis-tency, openness, treatment, two-way communication, and propriety of questions) concern the interpersonal treatment of the applicant throughout the selection pro-cess, especially during the administration of the selection measures. These Social higher-order factor subscales have serious implications for disparate treatment claims (e.g., inconsistency in the way individuals are treated, impropriety of ques-tions asked). Gilliland (1993) offered some examples of research on Social higher-order factor subscales that detailed practical methods for manipulating the interpersonal aspects of the selection process to bolster fairness reactions. This re-search will be discussed with the presentation of practical methods for incorporat-ing procedural justice below.

One all-encompassing step to take when attempting to cover possible proce-dural justice rule violations in this area would be for employers to thoroughly train

TABLE 1
Structure Higher-Order Procedural Justice Rules
and Incorporation Methods

Procedural Justice Rule and Sample Questions from the SPJS	Possible Methods for Incorporating Procedural Justice Rule
Job-relatedness–predictive: Doing well on this test means a person can do the [insert job title] job well.	Use of selection procedures based on a valid job analysis.
	Use of subject matter experts (job incumbents and supervisors) to develop selection instrument.
	Informational letter/flyer to candidates briefly describing job-relatedness of the selection procedures and how they were developed.
	Use of work-sample tests, interviews, and cognitive tests with relatively concrete item-types.
	Avoidance of personality, biodata, and cognitive tests with relatively abstract item-types.
Information known: I understood in advance what the testing process would be like.	Give applicants informative job announcements describing the steps involved in the selection process.
	Give applicants a way to contact the organization to obtain more information about the selection process.
Chance to perform: I could really show my skills and abilities through this test.	Use of work-sample tests (applicants actually performing tasks completed on the job).
	Use more than one job-related selection measure (if feasible and if related to the job) (e.g., written exam, structured interview, work sample, etc.).
Reconsideration opportunity: There was a chance to discuss my test results.	Incorporate an optional review/discussion session.
	Announce precise instructions for applicants to schedule session.
Feedback: I had a clear understanding of when I would get my test results.	Give applicants informative job announcements and/or flyers that describe the time in which they will receive the results.
	Ensure staff and resources are available to score selection measures in a timely manner.
	Give applicants a way to contact the organization to obtain more information on timelines and feedback.

Note. All sample questions taken from the SPJS (Bauer et al., 2001).

116

the staff who are administering selection measures. For example, the administration of a written cognitive exam may include handing applicants their exam booklets, directing them to their seats, reading instructions verbatim to all applicants, and collecting booklets when applicants are finished. However, the administration of a structured interview may entail detailed questions relating to complex work behaviors. Interviewers or rating panels may need extensive training on assigning appropriate ratings to complex questions and answers and how to avoid falling victim to common rater errors (e.g., halo, horns, similar-to-me, overgeneralization). Interestingly, Werner and Bolino (1997) investigated U.S. Circuit Court cases surrounding employee performance evaluations and delineated factors that were related to a decision in favor of the employer. Two of such factors included performance evaluations that had written instructions provided to raters and agreement of evaluation ratings among multiple raters. It is possible that by adding similar structure to interviews or appraisal panels, employers could avoid not only perceptions of unfairness but also burdensome trips to court.

The standardization of administration must be stressed to avoid pitfalls of the consistency rule (Gilliland, 1993) and honesty, communication, and treatment of job applicants must be covered to avoid applicant perceptions of unfairness during the interpersonal interactions with administrators. One way to address openness and two-way communication could be to train selection process administrators on how to field questions appropriately and honestly during the administration. Selection staff can generate lists of possible questions and answers from past administrations to arm administrators with appropriate information. Mock selection measure administrations or observation of administrations conducted by more seasoned personnel could prove an excellent opportunity to train newer examination administrators. In addition, there should be one or more designated points in the selection process when applicants are asked whether they have any questions. Empirical findings (Lounsbury et al., 1989) link the provision of timely feedback to applicants concerning their test results with more favorable reactions to a testing process.

Gilliland's (1993) interpersonal treatment rule was operationalized in subscales as the individual perceiving himself or herself to be treated with respect and consideration. Research concerning interviews has also indicated that the warmth and thoughtfulness (Schmitt & Coyle, 1976), personable qualities (Liden & Parsons, 1986), and respectful treatment (Bies & Moag, 1986) had significant implications for applicants' expectations concerning job offers and acceptance of those offers (Schmitt & Coyle, 1976), general affect of the interview (Liden & Parsons, 1986), and perceptions of fair treatment during the interview (Bies & Moag, 1986). It is somewhat more difficult to make recommendations for this subscale because the way individuals construe respectful behavior is different from person to person and potentially varies across cultures (Morris & Leung, 2000). Although it is impossible to recommend a standardized set of polite behaviors for all situations, Lind and Tyler (1988) found that the criteria used in justice judgments of an evaluator's behavior were identified as benevolence, neutrality, and status recognition. It could therefore behoove test administrators to ensure that they remain neutral from applicant to applicant, avoiding favoritism toward certain groups and discrimination against others. Research is needed in this area to discern more precisely the behaviors that constitute politeness and fair treatment during the testing process.

CONCLUSION

In the SPJS, Bauer et al. (2001) presented a useful tool that allows practitioners to gauge the fairness perceptions of applicants participating in a selection process. As pointed out by the SPJS developers, "Valid and reliable measurement of the different procedural justice constructs can assist practitioners and researchers in more fully understanding the role that fairness plays among applicants in different selection situations" (p. 389). Bauer and colleagues also proposed that the SPJS offers a more systematic method for testing Gilliland's (1993) procedural justice rule model that could allow for comparison across studies.

Truxillo et al. (2002) followed up with a study that actually manipulated the amount of information given to candidates and assessed procedural justice with the SPJS subscales of job relatedness and feedback. They found that applicants who received more information had significantly higher perceptions of procedural justice than those who received less. Similar research should be conducted to identify practical methods for enhancing the fairness perceptions of a selection process by manipulating certain aspects of that process. Though some preliminary research has been conducted concerning applicant reactions to selection procedures and the social order variables (e.g., Arvey & Sackett, 1993; Iles & Robertson, 1997; Schuler, 1993) more specific investigations using the SPJS items could distinguish more precise methods for incorporating the rules and offer further support and a broader range of understanding to the interpersonal dynamics of selection processes.

The goal of this review has been to present a useful tool to practitioners, discuss how procedural justice rules relate to current legal issues and offer some practical recommendations for improving fairness perceptions in the selection process based on the scale descriptions and recent research. However, certain recommendations may not correspond or be feasible to the hiring needs of the individual organization.

REFERENCES

Adams, J. S. (1965). Inequity in social exchange. In L. Berkowitz (ed.), *Advances in experimental social psychology* (Vol. 2, pp. 267–299). New York: Academic Press.
Arvey, R. D., & Sackett, P. R., (1993). Fairness in selection: Current developments and perspectives. In N. Schmitt & W. Borman (Eds.), *Personnel selection* (pp. 171–202). San Francisco: Jossey-Bass.

Association of Mexican-American Educators v. State of California, 937 F. Supp. 1397 (N.D. Cal. 1996).

Association of Mexican-American Educators v. State of California, 231 F.3d 572 (9th Cir. 2000). 937 F. Supp. 1397 *et seq.*

Bauer, T. N., Truxillo, D. M., Sanchez, R. J., Craig, J. M., Ferrara, P., & Campion, M. A. (2001). Applicant reactions to selection: Development of the Selection Procedural Justice Scale (SPJS). *Personnel Psychology, 54,* 387–418.

Bies, R. S., & Moag, J. S. (1986). Interactional justice: Communication criteria of fairness. In R. J. Lewicki, B. H. Sheppard, & M. H. Bazerman (Eds.), *Research on negotiations in organizations* (pp. 43–55). Greenwich, CT: JAI Press.

The Civil Rights Act of 1964, 42 U.S.C. § 2000e, *et seq.*

Connecticut v. Teal, 457 U.S. 440 (1982).

Gilliland, S. W. (1993). The perceived fairness of selection systems: An organizational justice perspective. *Academy of Management Review, 18,* 694–734.

Gilliland, S. W. (1994). Effects of procedural and distributive justice on reactions to a selection system. *Journal of Applied Psychology, 79,* 691–701.

Greenberg, J. (1986). Determinants of perceived fairness of performance evaluations. *Journal of Applied Psychology, 71,* 340–342.

Greenberg, J., & Lind, E. A. (2000). The pursuit of organizational justice: From conceptualization to implication to application. In C. L. Cooper & E. A. Locke (Eds.), *I/O Psychology: what we know about theory and practice* (pp. 72–108). Oxford, England: Blackwell.

Iles, P. A., & Robertson, I. T. (1997). The impact of personnel selection procedures on candidates. In N. Anderson & P. Herriot (Eds.), International Handbook of Selection and Assessment (pp. 543–566). Chichester, England: Wiley.

Leventhal, G. S. (1980). What should be done with equity theory? New approaches to the study of fairness in social relationships. In K. S. Gergen, M. S. Greenberg, & R. H. Willis (Eds.), *Social exchange: Advances in theory and research* (pp. 27–55). New York: Plenum.

Liden, R. C., & Parsons, C. K. (1986). A field study of job applicant interview perceptions, alternative opportunities, and demographic characteristics. *Personnel Psychology, 39,* 109–122.

Lind, E. A., & Tyler, T. R. (1988). *The social psychology of procedural justice.* New York: Plenum Press.

Lounsbury, J. W., Borbrow, W., & Jenson, J. B. (1989). Attitudes toward employment testing: Scale development, correlates, and "known-group" validation. *Professional Psychology: Research and Practice, 20,* 340–349.

Morris, M. W., & Leung, K. (2000). Justice for all? Progress in research on cultural variation in the psychology of distributive and procedural justice. *Applied Psychology: An International Review, 49,* 100–132.

Ployhart, R. E., & Ryan, A. M. (1997). Toward an explanation of applicant reactions: An examination of organizational justice and attribution frameworks. *Organizational Behavior and Human Decision Processes, 72,* 308–335.

Schmidt, F. L., & Hunter, J. E. (1998). The validity and utility of selection methods in personnel psychology: Practical and theoretical implications of 85 years of research findings. *Psychological Bulletin, 124,* 262–274.

Schmitt, N., & Coyle B. W. (1976). Applicant decisions in the employment interview. *Journal of Applied Psychology, 61,* 184–192.

Schuler, H. (1993). Social validity of selection situations: A concept and some empirical results. In H. Schuler, J. L. Farr, & M. Smith (Eds.), *Personnel selection and assessment: Individual and organizational perspectives* (pp. 11–26). Hillsdale, NJ: Lawrence Erlbaum Associates, Inc.

Sheppard, B. H., & Lewicki, R. J. (1987). Toward general principles of managerial fairness. *Social Justice Research, 1,* 161–176.

Singer, M. S. (1992). Procedural justice in managerial selection: Identification of fairness determinants and associations of fairness perceptions. *Social Justice Research, 5,* 49–70.

Singer, M. S. (1993). *Fairness in Personnel Selection.* Aldershot, New Zealand: Avebury.

Smither, J. W., Reilly, R. R., Millsap, R. E., Pearlman, K., & Stoffey, R. W. (1993). Applicant reactions to selection procedures. *Personnel Psychology, 46,* 49–76.

Steiner, D. D., & Gilliland, S. W. (1996). Fairness reactions to personnel selection techniques in France and the United States. *Journal of Applied Psychology, 18,* 134–141.

Stone, E. F., & Stone, D. L. (1990). Privacy in organizations, theoretical issues, research findings, and protection mechanisms. *Research in Personnel and Human Resource Management, 8,* 349–411.

Thibaut, J. W., & Walker, W. L. (1975). *Procedural justice: A psychological analysis.* Hillsdale, NJ: Lawrence Erlbaum Associates, Inc.

Truxillo, D. M., Bauer, T. N., Paronto, M. E., & Campion, M. A. (2002). Selection fairness information and applicant reactions: A longitudinal field study. *Journal of Applied Psychology, 87,* 1020–1031.

Tyler, T. R., & Bies, R. J. (1990). Beyond formal procedures: The interpersonal context of procedural justice. In J. S. Carroll (Ed.), *Applied social psychology and organizational settings* (pp. 77–98). Hillsdale, NJ: Lawrence Erlbaum Associates, Inc.

Werner, J. M., & Bolino, M. C. (1997). Explaining U.S. Courts of Appeals decisions involving performance appraisal: Accuracy, fairness, and validation. *Personnel Psychology, 50,* 1–24.

THE PSYCHOLOGIST-MANAGER JOURNAL, 2005, 8(2), 121–130

II. LIVE FROM THE FIRING LINE: THE PRACTICE OF MANAGEMENT

Avoiding a "Pounding" in Employment Litigation: A Few Ounces of Prevention

Clement L. Glynn and Quin E. Marshall

Glynn & Finley, LLP

The article provides trial lawyers' insights into common workplace management issues that may stimulate avoidable complaints or become obstacles in defending an employer in litigation. It reviews and provides examples of problems in performance evaluation, inconsistent application of workplace conduct policies in diverse work environments, documentation of training and receipt of policies, and management of inappropriate behavior that can help or hinder a company's defense against inevitable employee claims. The importance of proper investigation practices is examined as it relates to fact finding, claim prevention and litigation appearance. These subjects are illustrated with examples of the authors' actual trial experiences in defending employers in various employment litigation contexts. Recommendations are provided on how to avoid these common management pitfalls and increase the employer's credibility and chances of prevailing when facing disgruntled employees in court.

The role of the Human Resource (HR) professional today too often resembles that of the frenetic plate spinners who regularly appeared on the Ed Sullivan Show. These acrobatic artists would start a plate spinning at the end of a swaying and flexible wooden stick, gradually increasing the number of simultaneously rotating plates to some staggering number. The trick was to run from plate to spinning plate to reenergize their rotations, lest they lose momentum and crash to the floor in an ignominious and shattering failure. Although HR professionals do not need nearly the foot speed or hand-eye coordination of these dervishes of the small screen, they

Correspondence should be sent to Clement L. Glynn, Glynn & Finley, LLP, 100 Pringle Avenue, Suite 500, Walnut Creek, CA 94596. E-mail: cglynn@glynnfinley.com

nevertheless have much on their plates, and often far too many plates, period. This brief article will discuss a few thoughts on how to limit the number of plates by some basic but useful ideas on how to avoid avoidable problems and how to position the employer to defend successfully against problems that invariably occur. Though stated as ideas for HR Professionals, these recommendations will also be relevant to psychologists with managerial or supervisory responsibilities.

As lawyers who have defended employment lawsuits for many years, the authors have seen certain types of problems recur. There are lessons to be learned from these experiences, and this article will attempt to share some of those lessons with the reader. Naturally, there is an essential disclaimer: the real world is never neat or orderly—and not nearly as predictable as the influence of gravity on spinning plates. Nevertheless, some general observations of the sort that follow may assist the reader in grappling with diverse problems and in developing responses that help achieve positive outcomes.

THE PROBLEM OF APPROPRIATE PERFORMANCE MANAGEMENT AND EVALUATION

If there is any one theme that pervades employment litigation, it is surely that an overly charitable performance evaluation will come back to haunt you. When coupled with supervisory neglect of daily, routine performance issues, it is a double dose of poison and a recipe for liability. Here's a common scenario: Jane has been employed in one of many mid-management positions at Widgets, Inc., for eight years. Her performance has consistently been no better than average, but she is friendly and personally well liked by both of her past supervisors, Steve and Bob, who always rated her performance as "exceeding" expectations. Now, Widget must reduce force in order to remain competitive in its markets, and directs its managers to evaluate carefully all positions and the employees in them in order to determine where reductions can most feasibly be made. Jane's new manager, Floyd, has just completed his first evaluation of her, and has rated her as "average" on most categories, and "below average" on some critical categories. Jane confronts Floyd and accuses him of sex discrimination. Steve and Bob both thought she was great, she says, and nothing about her performance has changed, so there is no other explanation. Floyd is flabbergasted because in his mind, he could have been even more critical of Jane's performance, and he refuses to change his evaluation. Aware that a force reduction is on the horizon, Jane immediately files sexual discrimination charges with the EEOC and the California Department of Fair Employment and Housing (DFEH). Her charge features the eight years of outstanding performance evaluations, and the claim that Floyd, a male, is the first manager to rate her "negatively."

Widget proceeds with its force reduction program, and Jane is an obvious candidate not only because of her performance, but because of her position. But the company hesitates, aware of her charges of discrimination. In discussions about whether Jane's job should be spared to avoid the appearance of retaliation, management discusses the merits of her claim. They know that Floyd has a spotless reputation and has given glowing performance evaluations to several female employees. They also know that both Steve and Bob have been counseled by their own supervisors about being too soft on performance management issues and seem to avoid giving employee feedback that could cause discomfort or hurt feelings. So, the company decides that the right thing to do is follow the objective force reduction plan, which happens to call for elimination of Jane's position.

Upon learning that she is to be terminated, Jane files new charges with the agencies contending that she has been retaliated against for having engaged in the "protected activity" of making charges of discrimination. The agencies issue "right to sue" letters to Jane, who hires one of the top employment lawyers in town and files suit against Widget for sex discrimination and retaliation. Because of the proximity in time between Jane's discrimination complaint and her termination, and the fact that her complaint was discussed when termination decisions were made, even though it was not the basis of the termination decision, there is an automatic suggestion of retaliation, so the judge allows the case to go to trial. Lots of money is spent on the case. Employee morale goes down as rumors about the case circulate. Other performance-deficient or force-reduced employees get ideas about the potential for their own cases. And the list goes on.

Some variation on the above scenario happens every day. Certainly Jane could bring charges even without the history of favorable performance evaluations, but the credibility of her claims is significantly strengthened by those inflated evaluations. The fact is that Jane's performance had not changed—it was always marginal. What changed was her manager. Floyd was the first manager to evaluate her objectively. Prior managers had given her undeserved positive evaluations because she was nice, and because they wanted to be popular rather than effective supervisors.

This dynamic of inflated performance evaluations is very human and understandable, but very dangerous from a risk management standpoint. There are many reasons this occurs. A manager may lack the courage to deliver bad news to an employee with whom he or she wishes to remain "friendly." The manager may believe that by giving a more positive evaluation than is justified, he or she can better motivate the employee. Or the manager may be influenced by understandable—but ultimately irrelevant—considerations such as trying to get the employee the highest possible raise because of special personal needs of the employee. Whatever the reason, inflated performance evaluations are *always* ill-advised. When Jane's lawyer is constructing his case, he will feature the prior evaluations. He will argue that Jane's performance did not change (true), but all of a sudden, she is "inexplicably" downgraded by the company. And, he will argue that once Jane was brave enough to challenge Floyd's obviously biased evaluation, the company responded by firing her—a clear act of retaliation.

No matter how tenuous such a case, juries are comprised of people who work (or have worked) for a living. It is rare to find a group of prospective jurors that does not include a number of persons who feel that they themselves were the victims of unfair treatment at work, and such individuals are, no matter what they say during the jury selection process, assumed to be predisposed to side with the underdog—*i.e.,* someone like them. And, if Widget does not settle with Jane and loses at trial, the expenses can be enormous, not to mention the adverse effect such matters can have on the workplace.

All good HR professionals and psychologist-managers know the importance of giving and training supervisors to give objective and accurate performance evaluations, and most sophisticated companies have specific, objective guidelines. Nevertheless, these problems persist—indeed they are pandemic. So what to do? One technique that can be useful is to have training sessions in which role playing is used to illustrate the pitfalls of the overly charitable evaluation. In this manner, a company can demonstrate forcefully and realistically that the road to litigation hell is paved with good intentions. It has been our experience that once a manager participates as a witness in actual employment litigation, he or she learns indelibly these hard lessons. By including realistic role-playing in management training, an employer can attempt to change these practices and thereby help avoid the costs of learning the hard way.

THE PROBLEM OF INCONSISTENT ENFORCEMENT OF POLICIES

A related problem is the inconsistent enforcement of employment policies. Just as inconsistency in managing performance evaluations is a formula for litigation, so too is the inconsistent enforcement of employment policies generally. A fair disciplinary policy will usually allow for a case-by-case evaluation of misconduct to avoid unjustly harsh applications of any strict rule. But often the exceptions begin to swallow the rule until the rule itself ceases to exist.

This is difficult to manage, particularly in workplaces with a variety of work environments. For example, some companies have both industrial facilities and professional offices in one location, where the standards of courtesy and social interaction can be very different. It would not be uncommon for such a company to have one standard policy governing all employees regarding acceptable workplace behavior. But often its application to an issue such as the management of workplace banter between coworkers is very different depending on whether the employee is a member of a maintenance crew in the industrial section of the facility or an office worker in the administration building. What passes for acceptable in the welding yard might not go over so well at the fax machine. Right or wrong, that is usually true, until someone gets a bad performance review, or has a conflict with a supervisor or a coworker, or is reprimanded for misconduct, and starts to feel adversarially toward the company. Then the office worker disciplined for telling potentially offensive jokes complains that he has been subjected to disparate treatment, as evidenced by the permissive view taken of far more questionable talk in the field. Or an industrial worker facing discipline for attendance problems suddenly develops a sensitivity to rough talk and goes on stress disability, claiming to have been traumatized by years of offensive language (which, rest assured, some other employee will corroborate). In both scenarios, the company's position is harmed by having allowed different standards for application of one policy to exist. In practice, it is not necessarily realistic to expect employees in such different work environments to behave uniformly. But it is reasonable to expect management to respond to policy violations consistently, no matter who the offender.

THE PROBLEM OF PROVING EMPLOYEE RECEIPT
OF POLICY DOCUMENTS AND TRAINING

Another remarkably common mistake is the failure to document adequately the receipt by an employee of various crucial employment terms and guidelines. By taking some very elemental steps an employer can vastly improve its ability to avoid litigation or at least to maximize its chances of prevailing should litigation be filed. At the head of this list is ensuring, to the extent possible (for example, barring a collective bargaining agreement), that each employee *signs* a document acknowledging that he or she is employed "at will." "At will" means that the employee is not being hired for any specified term, and that the employer retains the right to terminate the employee at any time and for any reason. By the same token, the employee is not committing to the employer for any particular term and may choose to leave at any time, without sanction. This is the default and a dominant form of employment in California (California Labor Code 2005, § 2922), and many employers provide new employees with policy materials so advising them. Better yet is the inclusion of an agreement on the employment application, right above the applicant's signature line, acknowledging that if employment is offered, the applicant understands and agrees that it will be "at will" and that no other arrangement is authorized absent a separate written agreement signed by an officer of the company. In the State of California, for example, such a provision virtually cuts off all claims that the employee has an *implied* employment agreement requiring "good cause" for termination. Yet it is stunning how often employers do not take this simple step or otherwise require that employees sign a form acknowledging receipt and understanding of employment policies. Where such failure occurs, the employee is much freer to claim that he or she was not so advised and that he or she understood that termination could only occur if there was "good cause"—a much higher legal bar for the employer to overcome in wrongful termination litigation.

A related point concerns company workplace rules or training. Most sophisticated companies have some form of written guidelines given to employees that define accepted workplace behaviors. These may include, for example, guidance on what type of conduct is prohibited by the company's sexual harassment policy, or what sort of business gratuities are prohibited by the company's conflict of interest policy, and the like. Often these materials are provided to new employees at the time of hiring, followed by periodic updates as policies evolve. Too, it is common today to have actual classroom or computerized training modules on these subjects. In the event of a lawsuit, it may be crucial for the employer to be able to prove that the employee received certain of these materials or training. Yet all too often, tangible proof of receipt or participation is not there. By the simple expedient of requiring employees to sign an acknowledgment of receipt of such materials or training, the employer can establish important documentation that may be crucial in defending a later claim.

In a recent case defended by the authors (*Kennedy v. Chevron U.S.A., Inc.,* 2003), the plaintiff was a 20-year employee of a major corporation who was fired for accepting personal favors from a contractor doing business with the employer. The plaintiff had become friendly with an employee of the contractor who agreed to bring a piece of heavy equipment to her home on a weekend to help her with a major landscaping project. In the employer's view, this was a clear violation of the company's conflict of interest policy and the decision was made, reluctantly, to terminate an otherwise valued employee. At trial, the plaintiff claimed that the employer's conflict of interest policies had not been communicated to her, and that she thought accepting a favor from a friend away from work and on his own time was permissible. Because the employer had written proof to the contrary, the reasonableness of plaintiff's account could be challenged. For example, the jury was shown several documents signed by the plaintiff and acknowledging receipt of the conflict of interest policy and its updates and it was further proved that she had attended a training seminar on the subject a short time before her violation. Although she still argued that the policy was unclear and that despite her signature acknowledging receipt and understanding of the policy she had in fact never read it, the jury was not persuaded and returned a verdict for the employer. All trials involve competing accounts of past events but when there are hard documents, the room for "spin" is dramatically reduced.

A PROBLEM IN DEFINING "HARASSMENT"

Another area for caution with respect to policy training has to do with overstatement of the definitions and potential consequences of such terms as "harassment" and "hostile environment." Quite often, to set clear workplace behavioral standards and safeguard itself from claims, an employer will have a "zero tolerance" policy regarding any conduct which could be perceived as "offensive" to others. That may be a prudent policy. However, the law is not that strict and conduct which violates such a policy would not *necessarily* violate the law. Antiharassment laws, such as the Federal Title VII of the Civil Rights Act of 1964 and California's Fair Employment and Housing Act (FEHA, 2005), require offensive conduct to be either severe or pervasive before a hostile environment is established. Isolated, sporadic or trivial infractions are not a basis for liability under the law, although such conduct may very well be a basis for discipline under the company policy.

This difference between what is punishable under company policy and what is punishable under the law gives the employer a buffer zone in which to catch and address unacceptable workplace conduct before it can become a legal violation; this is desirable. But employee harassment training sessions and materials all too often fail to make this distinction clear, leaving employees with the impression that hearing a single offensive utterance gives them a legal claim against the company. In short, it is wise practice to sensitize employees to the types of conduct which will not be tolerated in the workplace but it should be done in a way that does not cause employees to perceive *legal violations* in every company policy infraction, no matter how small.

SOME PROBLEMS WITH WORKPLACE INVESTIGATIONS

One of the most crucial and tricky areas in avoiding litigation is the workplace investigation of employee complaints. These may be triggered in a variety of ways ranging from a direct complaint to a manager, an employee "hotline," or the HR Department itself, or in response to charges filed by the employee with a governmental agency. No two situations are identical, but some generalizations apply.

First, the investigatory process must be conducted with an eye towards determining the truth rather than placating the complaining employee or protecting the charged party. This perhaps sounds obvious but many regard these investigations as defensive in nature—that is, an effort to support the employer's side or just protect the company's reputation. Such a view misses the essential point that the employer's interests are best served by identifying and putting a stop to unacceptable workplace behaviors as soon as possible. The costs of not doing so can be staggering.

Second, it is vital that the person(s) conducting the investigation have no stake in the outcome. In other words, they must not be implicated in any sense by the charges. In today's world, it is not uncommon for members of the HR department themselves to become the object of charges by disgruntled employees who may view them as "shills" for management. In such cases, consideration should be given to bringing in investigators from other parts of the company, or, if necessary, from the outside. By so doing, an employer can preserve both the fact and appearance of objectivity.

Third, it is important that the investigator obtain, whenever possible, the claimant's agreement with the scope of the investigation and input as to potential sources of evidence. For example, the investigator may conduct an initial interview with the claimant to identify the issues and potential witnesses. Before embarking on the investigation, the investigator should write out his or her understanding of the charges and show that to the claimant for confirmation that the investigator has captured the issues correctly and completely. The investigator should encourage the claimant to submit his or her own written statement of the issue if desired and, where practicable, obtain the claimant's signature on the description of the scope of the complaint. In this manner, the investigator can head off a later argument by the claimant that the investigator missed the point or skewed what he or she was told by the claimant. By using this simple technique, the investigator will establish credibility with the claimant and, should there later be litigation, with the jury. This task has to be handled with finesse, so as not to intimidate or discourage employees from coming forward or proceeding with investigations. But the more proof of the claimant's agreement with the scope of the complaint, the better for avoiding the inevitable attempts to expand the claim if the matter ends up in litigation.

Fourth, it is crucial that there be consistency of the investigatory process. No two investigations are identical and to some extent the process must be adapted to the circumstances. It would be unrealistic to suggest, for example, that every investigation shall include at least five interviews or any other such formulaic approach. However, the more uniform the approach, the easier it will be to defend against later charges that the investigation was inadequate. Thus, the employer should develop a standard but adaptable protocol to guide investigations of employee complaints. This is particularly important when inquiries are conducted by members of management who are not necessarily trained in investigation techniques.

Under federal and state employment laws, such as Title VII of the Civil Rights Act of 1964 and California's FEHA (2005), courts routinely hold that an employee who unreasonably fails to provide his or her employer with notice of the claim and an opportunity to investigate limits his or her rights to recover. But that crucial defense for the employer will only apply where the employer's investigatory practices are reasonable. In other words, the law does not require an employee to give the employer an opportunity to investigate unless there is evidence that the employer would have conducted a reasonable investigation if given the chance.

Fifth, although perhaps a truism, it is worth stating that each step of the investigator's process should be fully documented. Notes should be taken during interviews of witnesses and documentation of the witness' agreement with the accuracy of the content of the notes can be invaluable in dealing with flawed memories and changed stories at trial. Generally speaking, assuming a competent and sophisticated investigator, the handwritten notes (or other contemporaneous records) of interviews should be retained rather than discarded after the final report is prepared. Witnesses should be informed how to submit subsequent information to the investigator if necessary, so no one can claim there was insufficient opportunity to share relevant information. This helps show the depth of the interviewer's efforts and these contemporaneous documents will often be given more credence by a jury than the final report which may be viewed as the sanitized and selective assemblage of the employer's story. Often the notes of the interview(s) with the claimant are among the most important documents in a case. If the employee has not yet "lawyered up" he or she may be less guarded and may provide more candid statements that are closer to the truth than what eventually is presented at trial.

Sixth, at the end of the investigatory process, it may be appropriate to advise the claimant regarding the evolved scope of the investigation and to give the claimant a last opportunity to provide input, suggest other witnesses who should be interviewed or other documents that should be reviewed. In this manner, the investigator can head off the common argument by claimants that the investigator failed to look into areas that should have been examined were there truly a good faith effort to learn the truth. As with all such interactions, it is best to have a written acknowledgement by the employee of these final discussions.

Finally, when the investigation is concluded, someone other than the investigator should make any decision as to how to respond to the employee's complaint based on the results of the investigation. The employer should then advise the employee of its determination, both orally and in writing. The oral discussion with the employee should include the investigator and at least one member of the employee's immediate management. The purpose of such meeting is not to debate the findings but to advise the employee in a personal way of the determination. If the employee's complaint is found to be without merit, this will provide the employee with one final chance to raise any further information he or she feels should be considered. If the complaint is found to be valid, the meeting can describe for the employee the steps being taken by the employer to respond to the problem. For example, in the case of confirmed sexual harassment by a coemployee, if employee discipline privacy policy permits, the employer may choose to advise the claimant that the harasser is being terminated; if more appropriate under the circumstances, that he or she is being relocated so that workplace contact with the claimant will be avoided; or that other discipline dictated by the company's policy is being undertaken. The face-to face-meeting is also an opportunity to reinforce the employer's commitment to workplace equity issues, the importance of confidentiality, and the like. Importantly, regardless of the determination of the merit of the complaint, management should take the opportunity at the meeting with the employee to stress its support for the company's antiretaliation policies and urge the employee to report immediately any retaliatory fallout for having brought a complaint forward.

After the meeting, the employer should provide the employee with a written response reflecting the employer's conclusions (but not the details of witness interviews) to avoid any possible misunderstanding and to preempt any claim by the employee that the employer was vague or under-communicative regarding its determination.

CONCLUSION

In today's workplace, there are many who seek to disrupt the spinning plates referred to earlier. Those whose job it is to keep the plates spinning without apparent effort have a much greater ability to do so by following some of the very basic concepts discussed above. The Ed Sullivan Show and similar variety programs are parts of history but the challenges of employer-employee relations are here to stay.

REFERENCES

California Labor Code § 2922 (2005). Retrieved June 16, 2005, from http://www.leginfo.ca.gov/cgi-bin/displaycode?section=lab&group=02001–03000&file=2920–2929

Civil Rights Act of 1964, Title VII, 42 U.S.C. § 2000e et seq.

Fair Employment and Housing Act, California Government Code § 12940 et seq. (2005)

Kennedy v. Chevron U.S.A., Inc., Contra Costa Superior Court Case No. C01–03963. (2003)

THE PSYCHOLOGIST-MANAGER JOURNAL, 2005, *8*(2), 131–140
Copyright © 2005 by the Society of Psychologists in Management

How to Use Documentation to Decrease the Likelihood of Litigation

Eric J. Sidebotham
Attorney-at-Law

Discrimination lawsuits can be a plague to employers. Proper documentation of the employment relationship is an important means of avoiding these lawsuits or defending against them. This article outlines some of the more important issues related to proper and effective ways for an employer to document the employment relationship. For example, as discussed in detail in the article, the burden to prove that employment discrimination did not occur can fall on the employer. The article briefly discusses several recent illustrative cases and points out the pitfalls made by employers in those situations. Although not intended to be a comprehensive study of all documentation necessary, the article discusses important documentation issues in the employment cycle, from the posting of a job advertisement to the termination of an employee.

Documentation of the employment relationship is important for one basic reason: documentation can provide an employer with tangible evidence to present to the judge or jury to demonstrate the fairness of the employer's actions in defense of a lawsuit. This article will outline some of the aspects of the employment relationship that should be documented. It is not intended to cover every possible situation. Competent legal counsel should be sought for advice about anything an employer should or should not document.

This article will discuss, from a legal perspective, the important points of documenting a relationship, with some practical suggestions and recommendations for the human resources (HR) professional. The first part of this article discusses some recent discrimination cases that, in some fashion, turned on the question of documentation—or a lack thereof. Next, the article will address several important events of the employee–employer relationship and identify some important things to document, including job announcements, application and selection documenta-

---

Correspondence should be sent to Eric J. Sidebotham, Attorney-at-Law, A Professional Corporation, 520 Calle Viento, Morgan Hill, CA 95037. E-mail: eric.sidebotham@verizon.net

tion, offer or engagement letters, performance reviews, harassment or discrimination complaints and investigations, and, finally, discipline.

As a lawyer, the worst thing I can hear from an HR professional who is seeking advice regarding a potential or actual employment lawsuit is that there is little or no documentation to support the challenged employment action. This article is intended to help the HR professional understand the role that documentation may play in the litigation context and expose some vulnerabilities resulting from a failure to document things properly.

CASES IN REVIEW

The first place to start is with a brief analysis of selected case law. Documentation of some particular aspect of the employment relationship has played a pivotal role in each of the following cases.

Exceptions to Policy

In *US Airways v. Barnett* (2002), the issue the United States Supreme Court was deciding was whether the *Americans with Disabilities Act of 1990* (ADA) required an employer to reassign an employee as a reasonable accommodation if the reassignment violated the employer's established seniority policy. Although the Court held that the employer was not obligated to reassign the employee, it opened a door by saying that an employee could prevail if he or she could present evidence that demonstrated that reassignment was nonetheless reasonable.

The evidence the employee needed to prevail in this factual situation would have been that US Airways had allowed numerous exceptions to its established seniority policies such that one more exception would not have had any real impact on the policy. Thus, to defend such an action, an employer must carefully document not only its polices (like its seniority policy) but also its consistent implementation of its policies. Any exceptions should also be carefully recorded, and the employer should have good reasons for the exceptions.

Performance Issues

The Ninth Circuit Court of Appeals, in *Fulkerson v. AmeriTitle, Inc.* (2003), reinstated a discrimination lawsuit that a former employee filed because it found the employer's proffered nondiscriminatory reason was pretextual. In that case, the employee was terminated shortly after she disclosed the fact that she was pregnant. The employer argued that it had legally terminated the plaintiff based on performance issues: she lied about being ill in order to get time off. The Court found, however, that the employer had not documented any performance-related reasons for termination, and thus reinstated plaintiff's lawsuit.

This case demonstrates not only the type of documentation an employer should collect, but also the timing in which it should be collected. The concern was that there were no documented prior performance reviews. Instead, it appeared as though AmeriTitle had raised performance problems only as a defense to a claim of discrimination. AmeriTitle simply had nothing to support its claim of prior performance problems.

Another example of the importance of documentation of performance can be found in *Mandell v. County of Suffolk* (2003), a discrimination and retaliation case in which the Second Circuit Court of Appeals cautioned that an employer may not solely rely on wholly subjective and unarticulated standards as a basis for its promotion decisions. In *Mandell*, the employer cited vague and general criteria of a "positive image" for not promoting the plaintiff, even though there was evidence that the decision makers preferred one protected category to another. The Court overturned summary judgment for the employer, stating that a reasonable juror could find the decision not to promote the plaintiff was based on religious discrimination.

Here, the employer's problem was that the documentation it did prepare was not very well thought out. In addition, it appeared as though the employer had something of a practice related to promotion (i.e., a positive image) but did not apply that practice to members outside the protected classification. For obvious reasons, the employer here was not able to document its even-handed application of its practices.

Deviations from Policy or Practice

It is fair to presume that in legal actions in the wake of these cases, employees may try to use any deviations from established policies and practices against their former employers. Failure to follow policies and practices can result in compromising them. It is, therefore, paramount for an employer to take considerable care in consistently documenting every important aspect of the employment relationship. In other words, an employee will have more difficulty arguing that the employer deviated from a policy or practice if the employer properly papered its trail. In certain circumstances, an otherwise consistent practice can rise to the level of being an implied policy. Deviation from the practice may also act as the basis for a discrimination action. For example, if an employer never conducts employee performance evaluations but then gives one performance evaluation and uses it as the basis for terminating someone of a protected classification, the employer may have a difficult time defending the resulting discrimination lawsuit.

OTHER EXAMPLES AND RECOMMENDATIONS

The importance of appropriate documentation illustrated by these cases applies to other employment events, starting with a description of the job and records of how it is advertised.

Job Description and Advertising Records

Before a decision is made to hire someone, an assessment of the requirements of the particular position should be carefully undertaken. Employers should document a description of the duties of the position, the hours to be worked, and any minimum qualifications such as education and experience. If it is an existing position, the old documentation should be reviewed to be certain that the job description matches the position as it currently exists and the qualifications are consistent with the individual(s) who have previously filled the position.

An employer can defend disability discrimination lawsuits by showing that the employee was unable to perform the essential functions of the job with or without a reasonable accommodation. Thus, identification of what is and is not an essential function is crucial. There may be no better way to demonstrate the essential functions of the job than by providing a well thought-out job description (based on job analysis) that was prepared *before* the position was even advertised. Again, this is another area where the timing of the documentation is important.

The employer should also take effort to insure that the advertisement itself complies with state and federal discrimination laws. Employers should refrain from disseminating any advertisement that expresses any preference, limitation, or specification as to any protected classification, directly or indirectly. For example, avoid using words that indicate a preference for one gender over another, or a preference for married or single, or young or old applicants.

A record of the text of the advertisement and of the locations where the advertisement is placed should be maintained. In responding to a complaint of discrimination over the search and selection process, it can be helpful if the job description, copies of advertisements, and a record of the locations in which the advertisements were placed are kept along with the applications that are received.

Application and Selection Materials

The law requires that employers preserve certain data related to their employees. Under California's Fair Employment and Housing Act of 1995 (FEHA, 2005), employers must keep applications, employment referral records, resumes, and other job inquiries for a set period of time. The ADA (1990) also requires employers to maintain certain records. In addition to the requirement that the records be kept for a given period of time, the Equal Employment Opportunity Commission (EEOC) and California Department of Fair Employment and Housing (DFEH) can request information about the applicant pool when investigating a claim of hiring discrimination. When an investigation takes place, the employer might have difficulty accurately reconstructing the recruitment for a particular job or job category if the records are not properly organized and preserved.

Everyone understands that job applications are used to evaluate potential employees. Applications can also be used as a tool to notify the applicant that the position is at-will, that the job is subject to an agreement to arbitrate, and that the employer may conduct a background check. Applications are even used on occasion to inform the applicant that employment will be subject to passing a medical examination or drug test.

As with the job advertisement, interview questions should be job-related and should refrain from expressing any preference as to any of the protected categories, directly or indirectly. Often applicants will provide unsolicited information about a protected category during the interview. For example, the applicant may refer to his or her spouse or children. When this occurs, the interviewer should steer the subject in a new direction and never write the information down. Moreover, the information should not be taken into consideration when the hiring decision is made.

The employer should make certain that the interviewers are trained not to collect information that is illegal to obtain in an interview or indicate a preference for or against any protected category. For example, there could be a negative inference of age discrimination if the interviewer were to write "energy level of a man half his age," while interviewing a mature gray-haired man. Such a notation could be very damaging in an age discrimination lawsuit, as well as in an EEOC investigation related to age discrimination—even if it the investigation is related to some other applicant. In any event, the notes taken by interviewers should be preserved, along with the applications.

Offer Letters

Employers should be careful to continue all of the diligent work that went into the advertising and interviewing process when the successful applicant is notified that he or she has been chosen for the job. Offer letters should refrain from language that undermines the at-will relationship and should also be specific as to any prerequisites to the final employment of the applicant. For example, if the final acceptance of the offer is subject to successful drug testing or medical examination or the execution of an arbitration agreement, the condition should be noted in the offer letter. Any applicable probationary period should also be specified in the letter. The terms of the new employee's benefits, especially relocation benefits or sign-on bonuses, should be set out in the letter. Lastly, a signature line for the applicant indicating his or her acceptance of the terms in the offer letter is a wise thing to include.

Once an individual is hired, it is important to make sure that all of the agreements between the employer and employee, such as a nondisclosure, invention assignment or arbitration agreements, are promptly executed. Sometimes employers will ask a new hire to sign an acknowledgement that the employee has received, has read, and agrees to be bound by the employee handbook. Additional information on preventing sexual harassment can be provided at the outset. The EEOC and DFEH have very good handouts for this purpose.

Performance Reviews

Creating and maintaining a consistent practice of conducting performance reviews is the next step for the properly documented employment relationship. Periodic, candid performance reviews often are a valuable resource in the defense of employment litigation. However, sporadic or less than candid reviews (especially inflated ones), can cause serious problems in defending employment lawsuits.

HR professionals should understand that some employees are aware that once they make a claim of discrimination or harassment, the employee might be entitled to additional protection under retaliation laws. Often, less than meritorious discrimination claims surface once an employee becomes aware that his or her performance is a cause of concern. If there is no written record of performance problems for the employee prior to the original claim of discrimination, there can be a question of fact as to whether the employer's claim of deficient performance is merely retaliation in response to a claim of discrimination. Again, the timing of documentation is almost as important as its content.

For example, the Court in *Bell v. Clackamas County,* 341 F.3d 858, 866 (9th Cir. 2003), found that the temporal proximity between the protected activity (such as making a claim of discrimination) and the adverse employment action, combined with management's alleged hostility, provided "strong circumstantial evidence" of retaliation. To make matters worse, management did not generate any notes from an irregularly scheduled meeting to discuss the plaintiff's alleged performance issues.

Performance problems that are documented prior to an initial claim of discrimination can demonstrate the employer's perception that there was a performance problem preceding the employee's claim of harassment or discrimination.

Harassment and Discrimination Complaints

Another area where documentation can be important is the handling of harassment and discrimination complaints. Employers are generally required to conduct an internal investigation in response to complaints of harassment of any protected classification. In *Casenas v. Fujisawa USA, Inc.* (1997), the court published its opinion in this sexual harassment case not based on a landmark legal principle but rather because the employer's conduct was a textbook example of how an employer should respond to a claim of harassment. The court was impressed by the documentation related to the Fujisawa's internal investigation. To follow the lessons taught by *Casenas,* prudent employers will conduct internal investigations immediately after they become aware of any workplace misconduct.

Employers should establish a written procedure for receiving complaints. Even though employers can request that complaints be made in writing, verbal complaints cannot be ignored. Verbal reports should be treated the same as written ones. The reason is that employees will often complain verbally to their manager or supervisor instead of submitting written reports to the departments designated for receiving such complaints. Managers and supervisors should be trained to recognize complaints and to report them to the appropriate department for investigation.

Failure to be consistent in handling discrimination or harassment complaints can lead to claims of discrimination or retaliation. Also, the failure to conduct an investigation before terminating an employee for misconduct can appear unfair and act as a catalyst for suit. However, well-documented evidence of workplace misconduct can establish a good cause for termination and take the wind out of a claim of discrimination. In such circumstances, an employer must have a good faith belief that an employee is guilty of misconduct in order to terminate an employee. That good faith belief must be based upon substantial evidence gathered through an adequate investigation. According to the Court in *Cotran v. Rollins Hudig Hall International, Inc.* (1998), an adequate investigation is one that includes "notice of the claimed misconduct and a chance for the employee to respond" (17 Cal.4th at 108).

Investigation of Harassment and Discrimination Complaints

Prompt and reasonable investigations often result in favorable outcomes for the employer. Indeed, a well-designed and properly executed investigation is the cornerstone of an antiharassment policy. In *Holly D. v. California Institute of Technology* (2003), a case involving a claim of sexual harassment of an employee by her supervisor, the Court applauded the employer who promptly convened an investigatory committee that impartially interviewed every witness suggested by the victim or her accused supervisor.

Similarly, in the case *State Department of Heath Services v. Superior Court (McGinnis)* (2003), the California Supreme Court held that the defense of avoidable consequence was applicable to damages claimed under FEHA. To establish such a defense, an employer must prove the following: (a) the employer took reasonable steps to prevent and correct workplace sexual harassment, (b) the employee unreasonably failed to use the preventative and corrective measures that the employer provided, and (c) the reasonable use of the employer's procedures would have prevented at least some of the harm that the employee suffered. It is worth noting for the HR professional that the employer has the burden of production and persuasion as to each of these affirmative defenses it alleges in an employment discrimination lawsuit.

To prove this defense, an employer must carefully develop an anti-sexual-harassment policy and then consistently document all of its actions taken to resolve and prevent sexual harassment in accordance with that policy. Gaps in the records and unexplained deviations from the policy will seriously undermine the defense. Furthermore, the employer must document a significant amount of negative information, that is, that the employee did not avail him or herself of the employer's policies. To establish this type of evidence, the employer will have to show that it regularly followed its procedures and, despite the fact that it followed the procedures, it has no record of plaintiff's involvement in the anti-sexual-harassment policies.

When learning that a work rule has been violated, the HR professional (or other designated person) who learns of the violation should memorialize the facts and circumstances under which he or she became aware of the violation and the names of any witnesses known at the time the violation was reported. This process is sometimes referred to as the initial intake.

After the initial intake, the employer should confirm the complaint in writing and determine whether further investigation is appropriate. Often this determination is made in consultations with attorneys. Factors that affect the employer's determination to conduct further investigation include whether there is potential work-related conduct that violates the law or a company policy, whether the employer has sufficient facts after conducting the initial intake to decide on a course of action without further investigation, whether an investigation is required by law or company policy, and whether the company generally investigates similar circumstances. If the employer chooses to investigate further, it should determine whether any interim action is appropriate.

If an employer decides to proceed with an investigation, the first step is to plan the investigation. This includes determining who will conduct the investigation, defining the scope of the investigation, determining the documents needed, identifying witnesses and the order of interviews, giving requisite notices, evaluating data, and reporting a conclusion.

There are many considerations to be taken into account in determining who should conduct the investigation, including in particular whether the person has good interviewing and documentation skills and a working knowledge of the employer's obligations regarding privacy. It is also important to choose someone who is not biased and who will not appear biased, either for or against the complainant or the alleged wrongdoer.

Once the plan for the investigation is in place, interviews should be conducted as soon as possible. All interviews should be in person and separately documented, including the date, time, and place of the interview, and the identity of those present at the time of the interview. The interviewer's notes should be clear, precise, and include all the facts. For example, the notes should reflect in detail not only everything that is said by a witness but also his or her demeanor, attitude, and appearance. The interviewer should ask open-ended factual questions of the interviewee to produce a description of what happened in his or her own words.

The investigator should also note the documents, including e-mails and voice mails, that he or she reviewed as part of the investigation. The report should draw attention to whether the complaint was substantiated by other witnesses, whether there are any discrepancies in the statements, and the credibility and veracity of the witnesses. Detailed summaries of each interview can be generated separately from the summary report.

The report itself should be considered a confidential document. The employer should keep the interview notes, lists of relevant documents reviewed, and final written summary of the findings and conclusions in a separate file that is confidential and secure. The results of the report should not be discussed with anyone who does not have a need to know, and distribution of the report should be restricted only to decision-makers and those who have a legal entitlement to receive a copy. If an employee conducted the investigation, the accused employee may have a right to receive a copy of the report. Once the investigation is completed, the employer must form a conclusion as to whether substantial evidence supports a finding that the alleged misconduct occurred. Substantial evidence does not mean conclusive proof.

Discipline

The last topic for this article relates to important documentation when an employee is disciplined. Of course a separate article could be written on this topic alone. The main purposes of discipline are to meet the company's legal obligations, to avoid further harm in the workplace, to avoid retaliation, to rectify problems and to be consistent with other cases, policies, and practices. All discipline should be documented and should include the action being taken and the basis for the imposition of discipline, with specific reference to the employer's policy or practice that was violated. Examples of disciplinary action include required training, verbal or written warning, suspension, probation, transfer, demotion, and termination.

Documentation of the discipline should be provided to the employee and, if possible, the employee should sign the document acknowledging receipt of it. If the employee refuses to sign the disciplinary documentation, the employer should note that the employee read and refused to sign it. If an investigation exonerates an employee, this should also be documented. The investigation notes and other documents should be preserved but kept separate from the personnel file.

It is very important that employers maintain consistency in disciplinary actions. Disciplinary actions should be as rational and fair as possible. A record of the other disciplinary actions taken can be helpful in showing this. An employer should take some care to keep track of all disciplinary actions. For that reason, many employ-

ers keep a database of disciplinary actions taken, and some also include all termi-
nations.

If there is a decision by the employer to deviate from the penalty called for by
polices and practices, or previously given to a similarly situated employee, the legitimate business reason for such deviation should be documented. For example, if
an employee misses 3 days of work and fails to call in, the employer may decide to
give the employee a second chance with a warning because the employee has no
history of absenteeism or tardiness. In such a case, it is important to document the
reasons that this employee only received a warning.

CONCLUSION

To conclude, appropriate documentation processes should be put in place and the
HR professional should be trained about these processes and the legal necessity for
them. This will prove valuable both in preventing lawsuits and in defending should
they occur. However, the difficult burden of following one's well-established policies and practices can be the key to preventing discrimination from occurring in the
workplace the first place.

ACKNOWLEDGMENTS

Eric J. Sidebotham is an attorney in San Jose. Mr. Sidebotham has represented employers and employees in litigation matters. This article is an adaptation of a presentation given by Sharon Kirsch, Esq. Michelle Tidalgo, Esq., an attorney working with Ms. Kirsch, also contributed to this paper.

REFERENCES

Americans with Disabilities Act, 42 U.S.C. § 12101, *et seq.* (1990).
Bell v. Clackamas County, 2003 WL 22025134 (9th Cir. 2003).
Casenas v. Fujisawa USA, Inc. 58 Cal.App.4th 101 (1997).
Cotran v. Rollins Hudig Hall International, Inc., 17 Cal.4th 93 (1998).
Fair Employment and Housing Act. Cal. Govt. Code §§ 12900 *et seq.* (2005).
Fulkerson v. AmeriTitle, Inc. No. 01–26163 (9th Cir. 2003).
Holly D. v. California Institute of Technology, 339 F.3d 1158 (9th Cir. 2003).
Mandell v. County of Suffolk, 316 F.3d 368 (2d Cir. 2003).
State Dept. of Heath Svcs. v. Superior Court (McGinnis) 31 Cal.4th 1026 (2003).
US Airways v. Barnett, 122 S.Ct. 1516 (2002).

THE PSYCHOLOGIST-MANAGER JOURNAL, 2005, *8*(2), 141–155

Managing an Employee Litigant: What to do to and How to Avoid Retaliation Claims

Donna Rutter

Curiale Dellaverson Hirschfeld & Kraemer, LLP

This article will provide an introduction to the federal laws governing retaliation claims, and will suggest 6 points essential to avoiding retaliation claims. Each point conveys invaluable advice about how to manage an employee litigant. This article can be useful in educating supervisors about what they can and cannot do while managing the employee litigant, how to deal with coworkers who are also aware of the lawsuit, how to get the best performance from this employee, and how to document the situation in such a way as not to fuel the employee's lawsuit but rather to provide the organization with a strong defense in the litigation.

What happens when one of your employees files a charge of discrimination with the Equal Employment Opportunity Commission (EEOC)? From that moment, interactions with that individual are never the same. Often, the employee becomes distant from management and preoccupied with making her or his case against the employer. The employee is often seen whispering to coworkers and writing copious notes in a spiral notepad when she or he should be working. Morale in the department begins to decline. Sound familiar?

Then, just when you think the situation could not possibly get worse, you open your mail and find a second charge of discrimination from the same employee, this time for retaliation. Now what will you do?

In 1998, the EEOC issued guidelines entitled "Section 8: Retaliation" as part of a Compliance Manual (guidelines). Significantly, the guidelines state

> The statutory retaliation clauses prohibit any adverse treatment that is based on a retaliatory motive and is reasonably likely to deter the charging party or others from engaging in protected activity. (Sec. 8, p. 13)

Correspondence concerning this article should be addressed to Donna Rutter, Curiale Dellaverson Hirschfeld & Kraemer, LLP, 727 Sansome Street, San Francisco, CA 94111. E-mail: drutter@cdhkk.com

This standard is very lenient. Thus, employers must understand the law on retaliation and implement safeguards to minimize these costly claims.

In 2002, Congress added additional protections against retaliation for employees who report about an employer's financial and accounting inconsistencies. The civil enforcement section of the *Sarbanes–Oxley Act* (2002), § 806, protects employees of public companies who suffer retaliation as a result of their disclosure of financial or accounting irregularities. Employers must become familiar with this new law and the expanded scope of employee protections against retaliation.

Retaliation is also prohibited under many state laws. This article does not endeavor to survey the laws of all 50 states or to provide an exhaustive list of employer obligations under those laws. However, readers should be aware that state retaliation laws exist and may provide broader coverage or protect activities not addressed here.

In this article, we provide a concise overview of the federal laws governing retaliation claims, and the points an organization should follow to avoid these costly claims.

FEDERAL LAWS PROHIBITING RETALIATION

Retaliation Involving Discrimination Claims

Title VII of the *Civil Rights Act of 1964*, the *Age Discrimination in Employment Act* (1967), the *Americans with Disabilities Act* (ADA; 1990), and the *Equal Pay Act* (1963) are the federal laws that prohibit retaliation by an employer, employment agency, or labor organization because an individual has engaged in protected activity. Protected activity consists of the following:

1. Opposing a practice made unlawful by one of the employment discrimination statutes (the opposition clause).
2. Filing a charge, testifying, assisting, or participating in any manner in an investigation, proceeding, or hearing under the applicable statute (the participation clause).

To maintain a claim for retaliation, a plaintiff must make the following showing, referred to as a *prima facie* case of discriminatory retaliation:

1. She or he engaged in an activity protected under [a discrimination statute].
2. His or her employer subjected her to adverse employment action.
3. There was a causal link between the protected activity and the employer's action.

Once a plaintiff establishes a *prima facie* case, the employer must then articulate a legitimate, nonretaliatory explanation for the action. If the employer successfully rebuts the *prima facie* case, then the burden shifts once again to the plaintiff to show the defendant's proffered explanation is merely a pretext for discrimination.

Retaliation Related To Disclosure of Financial and Accounting Irregularities

Section 806 of the *Sarbanes–Oxley Act* (2002) forbids retaliation against employees who file complaints or participated in proceedings against an employer accused of violating federal fraud or securities laws.

To be protected, the employee must reasonably believe that the conduct he or she reports violates federal fraud and securities laws and he or she must have filed a complaint with one of the following:

1. A federal agency.
2. A member of Congress or committee of Congress.
3. A person with supervisory authority over the employee.
4. Any person working for the employer who has the authority to investigate, discover, or terminate misconduct (such as corporate officers and managers).

The Act's civil provision is limited in important respects. It does not apply to non-publicly traded companies, and its protections only extend to activities related to a breach of federal fraud and securities laws. Interestingly, employees who report corporate fraud to the news media do not appear to be protected by the Act.

Broader damages for blowing the whistle.   The *Sarbanes–Oxley Act* (2002) offers a variety of legal remedies to whistleblowers who experience retaliation for sharing information about federal fraud and securities law violations. Specifically, employees who are subject to retaliation are entitled to any relief that would make the employee whole, including reinstatement, back pay with interest, attorneys' fees, and other related costs. Claims for compensatory damages are not capped under the statute, and may include relief for pain and suffering or emotional distress. The Act does not provide for the recovery of punitive damages. These remedies are broader than those offered under current California law in that they can now be awarded against individuals engaged in retaliation as well as the company. Significantly, these remedies are available to any employee who experiences any form of retaliation, not just termination.

No preemption.   The Act explicitly states that § 806 does not preempt existing state and federal protections for whistleblowers. Accordingly, employers must remain in compliance with existing whistleblower laws.

Criminal penalties for retaliation in all federal investigations. Section 1107 of the Sarbanes–Oxley Act (2002) imposes stiff criminal penalties for retaliating against whistleblowers under certain circumstances. It states

> Whoever knowingly, with intent to retaliate, takes any action harmful to any person, including interference with the lawful employment or livelihood of any person, for providing to a law enforcement officer any truthful information relating to the commission or possible commission of *any federal offense*, shall be fined …or imprisoned not more than 10 years, or both. (18 U.S.C. §1513[e])

The new criminal provision is *not* restricted to employees of public companies or limited to areas involving securities fraud. It extends to all investigations of any federal offense. Although the term *offense* generally refers to criminal conduct, employers should prepare for a generous construction encompassing all violations of federal law—civil and criminal—until courts clarify the meaning of the term. Accordingly, employers should assume that the provision applies to any investigation conducted by the EEOC, Occupational Safety and Health Administration and the National Labor Relations Board, and other federal agencies.

Some elements of the Act's criminal section are narrower than its civil provision. Section 1107 only protects "truthful information." Information which an employee reasonably believes is true but which is in fact false does not appear to be protected. Further, § 1107 only extends to disclosures made to law enforcement personnel. Although the Act defines law enforcement personnel broadly to include many "officers and employees of the federal government," actions taken on the basis of communications to supervisors and other agents of an employer do not trigger the provision.

EEOC Guidelines on Retaliation

Below, we summarize the significant sections of the EEOC guidelines (1998) regarding retaliation.

Basis for filing a charge. In Section 8-I B of the guidelines, the EEOC confirms that a charge of retaliation may be filed by an employee whether or not he or she also alleges he or she was treated differently because of a protected characteristic such as race or gender. Similarly, a charging party who alleges retaliation in violation of the ADA need not be a qualified individual with a disability.

The EEOC also clarifies that an employee can file retaliation charges even if the retaliation occurred after the employment relationship ended. For example, in *Robinson v. Shell Oil Company* (1997), the Supreme Court unanimously held that Title VII prohibits employers from retaliating against former employees, as well as current employees, for participating in any proceeding under Title VII or opposing any practice made unlawful by that Act. In *Robinson*, the plaintiff alleged his former employer gave him a negative job reference in retaliation for his filing an EEOC charge.

Examples of opposing discriminatory practices. An employee need not actually file a charge of discrimination with an outside agency. The EEOC guidelines provide that threatening to file a complaint with an agency is a form of opposition for purposes of establishing a retaliation claim. Similarly, a complaint or protest about alleged employment discrimination to anyone constitutes opposition. Opposition may also be nonverbal, such as picketing or engaging in a production slow-down.

A person is protected against retaliation for opposing perceived discrimination if she had a "reasonable and good faith belief that the opposed practices were unlawful " (Section 8-11.B.2). Thus, the retaliation provision can be violated even if the underlying challenged practice ultimately is found to be lawful.

Examples of participating in a proceeding. The antiretaliatory provisions apply to individuals challenging employment discrimination in EEOC proceedings, in state administrative or court proceedings, as well as in federal court proceedings, and to individuals who testify or otherwise participate in such proceedings. Although the opposition clause applies only to those who protest practices that they reasonably and in good faith believe are unlawful, the participation clause applies to *all* individuals who participate in the statutory complaint procedure.

What constitutes an adverse action. As mentioned previously, the most significant aspect of the guidelines is the adoption of an extremely lenient standard for what constitutes an adverse action. In addition to denial of promotion, refusal to hire, denial of job benefits, demotion, suspension, and discharge, the guidelines provide that the following are also adverse actions: threats, reprimands, negative evaluations, harassment, or other adverse treatment.

In the guidelines, the EEOC observes that "some courts have held that the retaliation provisions apply only to retaliation that takes the form of ultimate employment actions." Yet, the EEOC departs from those authorities, stating "such constrictions are unduly restrictive" (1998, Sec. 8, p. 13).

As discussed above, the EEOC's test is whether there was a retaliatory motive and whether the action was "reasonably likely to deter the charging party or others from engaging in protected activity" (Section 8-11.D.3). Unless the conduct is deemed a trivial annoyance or petty slight, it may constitute an adverse action.

The following examples are taken directly from the guidelines and illustrate the breadth of an adverse action:

Example 1—Charging Party (CP) filed a charge alleging that he was racially harassed by his supervisor and coworkers. After learning about the charge CP's manager asked two employees to keep CP under surveillance and to report back about his activities. The surveillance constitutes an "adverse action" that is likely to deter protected activity and is unlawful if it was conducted because of CP's protected activity.

Example 2—CP filed a charge alleging that she was denied a promotion because of her gender. One week later, her supervisor invited a few employees out to lunch. CP believed that the reason he excluded her was because of her EEOC charge. Even if the supervisor chose not to invite CP because of her charge, this would not constitute unlawful retaliation because it is not reasonably likely to deter protected activity.

Example 3—Same as example 2, except that CP's supervisor invites all employees in CP's unit to regular weekly lunches. The supervisor excluded CP from these lunches after she filed the sex discrimination charge. If CP was excluded because of her charge, this would constitute unlawful retaliation since it could reasonably deter CP or others from engaging in protected activity. (Sec. A. II. D.3., p. 13)

CASES WHERE RETALIATION WAS FOUND IN THE CONTEXT OF DISCRIMINATION

United States Supreme Court Decisions

Equal treatment, not preferential treatment.   In *Clark Community School District v. Breeden* (2001) the Court held that employers do not have to suspend a previously planned transfer of an employee upon discovering that a Title VII suit had been filed by that employee. The employer may proceed and act regarding that employee as previously planned. Such actions will not constitute evidence of retaliation. The Court also held that no claim for retaliation exists where a reasonable person could not reasonably believe that the basis for the complaint, upon which the alleged retaliation is based, violated Title VII.

In this case, the female plaintiff met with her male supervisor and another male employee to evaluate the psychological evaluation reports of four job applicants. The report for one of the applicants disclosed that the applicant had once commented to a coworker, "I hear making love to you is like making love to the Grand Canyon." At the meeting, the plaintiff's male supervisor read the comment aloud, looked at the plaintiff and said, "I don't know what that means." The other male employee said, "Well, I'll tell you later," and both men chuckled. The plaintiff later complained about the comment to the male who made the comment and to several of her supervisors. The plaintiff claimed that the comment constituted sexual harassment against her and claimed that she was eventually retaliated against for complaining about the male supervisor's comments. The plaintiff further alleged that she suffered adverse employment actions for complaining about the alleged harassment. She alleged that she was eventually transferred to a less desirable position after she complained about the alleged harassment.

The Supreme Court held that any punishment suffered by the plaintiff for complaining about the alleged sexual harassment by her male coworker did not constitute actionable retaliation because the underlying incident itself did not violate Title VII and the plaintiff's complaints, therefore, did not constitute protected activity. The conduct of the plaintiff's male coworkers at most constituted an isolated incident which could not be deemed sufficiently severe or pervasive to alter the terms and conditions of her employment. Further, the defendant company's stated intention to transfer the plaintiff expressed shortly after the lawsuit was filed did not establish a causal connection between the transfer and the lawsuit based on temporal proximity because the defendant was not served with the plaintiff's complaint until after the statement expressing the intention to transfer was made.

Court of Appeal Decisions

Court of Appeal decisions, unlike Supreme Court decisions, are not controlling in other jurisdictions. Nonetheless, they are binding in the area where the court sits, and opinions issued in one jurisdiction are likely to influence future decisions rendered in other parts of the country. The following Court of Appeal decisions illustrate current trends in retaliation law and answer questions not yet addressed by the Supreme Court.

Supervisors may be personally liable for retaliation.   In *Winarto v. Toshiba America Electric Components* (2001) the Court found that supervisors may be individually liable for retaliation under the California *Fair Employment and Housing Act* (FEHA, 2005).

In this case the plaintiff was laid off from her job. The plaintiff sued her employer and some of her managers and coworkers raising claims of illegal retaliation and civil rights violations. The plaintiff was a woman of Indonesian ancestry. She was well qualified for the job, she held degrees in relevant fields, and was more experienced for her job than most of the members of her work group.

Mr. Birtch, one of her supervisors, allegedly harassed her and she complained to another supervisor that Birtch had called her a lesbian and a virgin in front of other coworkers. Birtch continued to harass the plaintiff verbally and he also undertook a campaign of kicking the plaintiff many times. The plaintiff complained to her other supervisor, Taylor, but the kicking never stopped. Later that year, the plaintiff was transferred to another group and was placed under the supervision of supervisor Royer. Royer gave the plaintiff a mixed performance evaluation. The next year, after complaining about Royer, the plaintiff was transferred back to her original group and supervisor. The plaintiff began again to complain about Birtch's harassment. Later that year, the plaintiff was diagnosed with a back injury. A doctor wrote a note that sought to limit her lifting responsibilities but despite this her coworkers forced her to continue to move heavy computers. As a result, she reinjured her back, which caused her to miss work. The doctor sent a second note, more restrictive than the first.

The plaintiff complained to Taylor about other members of the work group besides Birtch who were harassing her about her back injury. The next year, Taylor gave her a performance evaluation with a low rating. Later that year, the plaintiff took a medical leave to have surgery on her ankles and 11 days after she returned she was laid off, partially because of her low performance rating by Taylor that year. Shortly after the reduction-in-force (RIF), the plaintiff filed two written complaints in response to the low performance evaluation, which she had received while on medical leave. In the complaints, she alleged that she had been discriminated against and harassed by Taylor and several coworkers and managers because she was a woman, a minority, and had suffered injuries that kept her away from work. Once the company received the complaints, it delayed the decision to terminate her pending an investigation and eventually decided to go forward with the layoff of the plaintiff.

The plaintiff sued for discrimination and retaliation and a jury awarded her damages. On appeal the Court held that manager Taylor's evaluations were retaliatory. And the Court held that Taylor could be held individually liable for retaliation under the FEHA.

Defining an adverse employment action. In the retaliation context, adverse employment action occurs when adverse treatment is reasonably likely to deter employees from engaging in protected activities. Under this standard, a hostile work environment may form the basis for a retaliation claim.

In *Ray v. Henderson* (2000), after the plaintiff complained about management's treatment of women employees, management eliminated employee meetings, eliminated its flexible starting time policy, instituted a lockdown of the workplace, and cut the plaintiff's salary. The plaintiff filed suit, complaining of a hostile work environment and retaliation. The Court in this case adopted the EEOC's standard that retaliation was actionable if it was reasonably likely to deter employees from engaging in protected activity. The plaintiff established a causal link between his protected activity, complaining about management's treatment of women, and the employment actions taken against him. Therefore, the plaintiff presented evidence that was sufficient to raise a genuine issue of material fact as to whether he was subjected to a hostile work environment.

Increased scrutiny of an employee. Lana Mockler was a Deputy Sheriff with the Multnomah County Sheriff's office. After she filed a sexual harassment complaint against a coworker, Mockler's supervisor told her she should "dot her i's and cross her t's." Mockler was thereafter subjected to increased disciplinary action, while other deputies were not disciplined for similar conduct. Additionally, Mockler did not obtain several positions she applied for and, in one instance, was told the position was "too politically sensitive a place for her" because she was a "political hot potato."

On another occasion, she was denied a coach position for new recruits because of the "big fiasco" involving the lawsuit. Mockler took a 3-month stress leave and eventually transferred to the Portland Police Bureau. She sued Multnomah County and two individual defendants for sexual harassment and retaliation and was awarded $195,000 in compensatory damages and $30,000 in punitive damages.

The Ninth Circuit affirmed the jury's verdict. As to the retaliation claim, the court found "the evidence presented by Deputy Mockler and by the defendants overwhelmingly demonstrates that the county failed to take effective remedial action to end the ...retaliation against Deputy Mockler" (*Mockler v. Multnomah County*, 1998, Sec. II [7] at 813).

Negative job references.   Barbara Hashimoto worked for the Navy as a budget analyst from April 1984 through June 1986. Hashimoto was terminated due to a RIF. Just prior to her termination, she initiated an administrative complaint claiming she was discriminated against because of her race and gender and because she met with an EEOC counselor. Specifically, she alleged she was improperly suspended on two occasions, denied a salary increase, and wrongly terminated through the RIF.

While her first complaint was pending, Hashimoto filed a second complaint in which she alleged that she received a negative job reference (when she applied for an Army job in 1988) from her prior supervisor in retaliation for filing her initial complaint.

The Ninth Circuit affirmed the district court's ruling in favor of Hashimoto on the grounds the Navy retaliated against her when it gave the Army a negative reference. The court rejected the Navy's argument that the negative reference could not constitute an adverse employment action because Hashimoto would not have obtained the job with the Army anyway. The court reasoned

> [T]he government's argument in this case fails to recognize the distinction between a violation and availability of remedies. [The supervisor's] dissemination of the adverse job reference violated Title VII because it was a "personnel action" motivated by retaliatory animus. That this unlawful personnel action turned out to be inconsequential goes to the issue of damages, not liability. (*Hashimoto v. Dalton*, 1997, at 676)

The Financial Consequences of Losing a Retaliation Lawsuit

Recent jury verdicts illustrate the potential risk in retaliation lawsuits. Because of the inherent nature of *retaliation claims*—alleging adverse action against individuals because of their invocation of legally protected conduct—some juries have returned substantial awards, consisting primarily of punitive damages.

For instance, in *Channon v. United Parcel Service* (2001), an Iowa jury awarded $527,872 in compensatory damages and $80.2 million in punitive damages to a manager who claimed she had been discriminated against because of her sex, and retaliated against when she complained about the discrimination. In *Breaux v. City of Garland* (1997) a Texas jury awarded $25 million in punitive damages to two police officers who claimed they experienced retaliation after they complained about politically motivated investigations into local politicians. In *Songco v. Century Quality Management., Inc.,* (1997), the jury awarded $4.5 million in punitive damages to a plaintiff who claimed he was fired in retaliation for reporting tax code violations, even though the jury determined that the plaintiff suffered only $35,148 in actual damages. The cases illustrate the willingness of jurors to award astronomical amounts in punitive damages to plaintiffs in retaliation cases, and reinforce the importance of avoiding retaliation claims.

Cases Where Employers Prevailed

Knowing what you can do is as important as knowing what you cannot do when managing an employee litigant. The following cases provide examples of employer actions that do not constitute unlawful retaliation, and clarify the types of employment actions that are likely to be upheld when applied to an employee who has exercised his or her rights.

Violations of company rules.   In 1993, U.S. Bank terminated Travis-Barker, a senior supervisor in its Seattle Eastlake Branch, for alleged irregularities in handling her own account. She sued the bank, alleging race discrimination and retaliation under Title VII. In support of its summary judgment motion, the bank introduced affidavits and bank records showing that Travis-Barker was suspended and ultimately discharged for a legitimate, nondiscriminatory reason: she was waiving overdraft fees on her own checking account in direct violation of bank policy. The Ninth Circuit affirmed the district court's grant of summary judgment because Travis-Barker offered no evidence that the bank's articulated reason for her termination was a pretext for discrimination (*Travis-Barker v. U. S. Bank, NA,* 1997).

Performance problems.   Alisa Huff filed a retaliation action against her employer, claiming that she was terminated in retaliation for filing an internal equal opportunity complaint. At trial, the evidence showed Huff's repeated problems with other employees interfered with her work performance and completion of assignments. The corrective action memos and discipline she received provided sufficient evidence that Huff herself contributed to the problems in her workplace atmosphere. Moreover, Huff failed to establish a causal link between the filing of her complaint and her discharge because the supervisor who terminated her did not know of her complaint. Finally, substantial evidence showed that her termination was the result of performance problems.

After Huff rested her case in a bench trial, the district court entered judgment in favor of defendants. The Ninth Circuit affirmed because there was no evidence of a causal link (*Huff v. Boeing Co., 1997*).

No duty to promote unqualified employees.   Ida Foster worked as a long-time employee of the Veteran's Administration Northern California Health Care System as a batch examiner in the Fee Service Section. Beginning in 1991, Foster applied for at least 10 job promotions or transfers. Her applications were all denied. In 1993, she began to file Equal Employment Opportunity (EEO) complaints, alleging discrimination regarding specific denials of jobs.

The district court granted the employer's motion for summary judgment because Foster's lack of qualifications for the position constituted a legitimate, non-discriminatory reason for not selecting her, and Foster failed to offer evidence that the employer's proffered reason was a pretext for retaliation (*Foster v. Brown,* 1998).

Corrective action as a defense.   Before discussing the facts and reasoning of *Casenas v. Fujisawa USA, Inc.* (1997), it is important to note the court's introductory remarks:

> We publish our opinion because Fujisawa's conduct is a textbook example of how to respond appropriately to an employee's harassment complaint. We do not know what more the employer could have done to accommodate Casenas, short of ceding its managerial prerogative to her. (1997, at 103)

Bernardine Casenas had been a sales representative for Fujisawa from 1986. She resigned in 1989 because she claimed the work environment became "intolerable" after she filed a sexual harassment complaint against her supervisor. On a motion for summary judgment, Fujisawa was able to prove that the following facts were undisputed: (a) Casenas had received an 8% bonus in 1988, (b) in 1989, she received a 7% bonus, (c) Casenas complained about her 1989 performance appraisal and the size of her 1989 bonus and the matter was reviewed and approved by different managers, (d) thereafter, Casenas complained for the first time that the evaluating supervisor had sexually harassed her, and (e) the sexual harassment complaint was investigated and the supervisor (who had since transferred) was given a warning letter and told not to have further contact with Casenas.

The Court of Appeal affirmed the lower Court's grant of summary judgment. The court rejected plaintiff's claim that the company had retaliated against her by not altering her performance appraisal and increasing her bonus. The Court found the company had legitimate reasons for its action and that Casenas had no facts to support an inference of "pretext."

SIX POINTS ESSENTIAL TO AVOIDING
RETALIATION CLAIMS

Once you understand the law on retaliation, you should then implement safeguards to minimize the risk that a retaliation claim will be brought against the organization. These claims are not inevitable. Moreover, even if a retaliation claim is filed, adherence to the following six points will enable the organization to defend itself against frivolous retaliation claims.

Point One: Train All Supervisors about Basic EEO
and Retaliation Policies and Procedures

Clearly, the most important step the organization can take to avoid retaliation claims is to make sure all supervisors understand what the law is in the areas of discrimination, harassment, and retaliation. Proper training will insure that supervisors do not take adverse actions against employees because those employees filed a charge of discrimination or participated in an investigation of discrimination. Similarly, training will illustrate how supervisors can still issue proper discipline, including discharge, of an employee who has violated the employer's policy, even though that employee has engaged in a protected activity. As the previous cases demonstrate, the courts will support an employer's right to discipline an employee, so long as the discipline is consistent with that given to noncomplaining employees. We recommend that a human resources representative monitor all discipline and other performance-related decisions involving employees who have filed discrimination claims to ensure there is no disparate treatment between employees who have made claims when compared to those who have not.

Training on retaliation issues should include, at a minimum, definitions of what constitutes "opposing an unlawful practice" and "participating in an investigation of unlawful practice." Further, supervisors should be taught not to make negative comments or job references about employees who file charges of discrimination or participate in a discrimination-related investigation. Similarly, supervisors must be aware that they cannot refuse to hire a worker because she had previously filed a charge of discrimination. Supervisors must also know that employees are protected from retaliation even when discrimination charges are untrue. In other words, employees still have the right to bring a charge, regardless of the ultimate merits of the case.

Finally, and perhaps most significantly in light of the EEOC's guidelines, supervisors must be educated about the broad meaning of "adverse activity." They must understand that repeatedly ostracizing an employee who has engaged in a protected activity may—without more—constitute an adverse action and should, therefore, be avoided.

Point Two: Treat All Employees the Same

It may seem axiomatic but management must impose both favorable and unfavorable treatment on employees equally, regardless of whether one employee has filed a frivolous charge of discrimination. If you must discipline an employee who has engaged in protected activity, then you must impose discipline that is *consistent* with that given to noncomplaining employees. As elementary as it may seem, managers must understand that similarly situated employees must be treated similarly. Otherwise, employers are setting themselves up for discrimination and retaliation claims.

Point Three: Advise Employees that Retaliation Will Not Be Tolerated

Include a statement prohibiting retaliation in all of your organization's nondiscrimination policies and complaint procedures. Such a statement should also appear at the bottom of any internal complaint forms your organization uses. Moreover, during an investigation of discrimination, always advise the complaining employee and all witnesses that retaliation is prohibited and will not be tolerated. If they believe they are being subjected to retaliatory conduct, they should report it immediately.

Point Four: Do Not Give Negative References Regarding Former Employees who Engaged in Protected Activity

Just because an employee leaves the organization does not mean that he loses his right to file a claim of retaliation for postemployment retaliation. The most common form of postemployment retaliation is the dissemination of negative information about a former employee to a prospective employer. To be safe, many employers choose not to give positive or negative information about *any* former employees, opting instead merely to verify their employees' last salary and positions held. We recommend a proactive approach of establishing a general policy that requires all employees to sign a release allowing you to give job references.

Point Five: Pay Attention to Documentation

Remember that any memorandum, e-mail, or correspondence about an employee may end up being disclosed in a lawsuit someday. Once an employee has filed a charge of discrimination, however, postcomplaint documents are more likely to be disclosed in a subsequent lawsuit.

Employers should follow three basic rules regarding documentation. First, in connection with an investigation of discrimination, obtain as much documentation as possible from all witnesses. Employee alliances can fluctuate over time, and it is critical to have the first story memorialized. Second, in connection with performance documentation, be consistent. Do not create excess documentation regarding an employee who has engaged in protected activity. It could look as if the company is trying to "paper" the complaining employee's file. Last, advise all supervisors and human resources personnel not to editorialize their views of a complaining employee's charge of discrimination any more than is necessary and to keep comments about performance as objective as possible. Otherwise, if there is a retaliation claim, those postcomplaint internal communications can be devastating to the employer's defense that the complaining party was treated consistently.

Point Six: Only Employees with a Need to Know Should Be Advised about an Employee's Charge of Discrimination or Harassment

The fewer the number of employees who know about another employee's charge of discrimination or harassment the better. If a supervisor takes an adverse employment action against an employee soon after the employee engaged in a protected activity, the judge's first question will be: "Did the supervisor know the employee had engaged in protected activity?" Whenever possible, the answer to that question should be "no." If a supervisor did not know about the protected activity, she could not have used that information in connection with the adverse action. Without the possibility of a causal link, the employee cannot state a *prima facie* case of retaliation.

CONCLUSION

Although it may be tempting to ignore an employee who has filed a frivolous charge of discrimination, the law and EEOC guidelines make it clear that such seemingly innocuous conduct could still create legal liability for retaliation. To combat these claims, employers must know the law and educate all supervisors about the law. Such training should minimize the number of retaliation claims your organization will receive, as well as heighten your ability to have the claims dismissed promptly and before the case goes to a jury.

Employers can also mitigate their exposure to retaliation claims by ensuring that work rules are enforced consistently. Employees who engage in protected activity do not become immune to normal work rules and professional expectations.

Like anyone else, they can be held to performance expectations and disciplined for improper conduct. However, it is imperative that employers apply their policies evenhandedly, and not single out employees who make complaints for unfavorable treatment.

Finally, employers should follow all of the six points for avoiding retaliation claims addressed in this article. It is not necessary to learn a labyrinth of legal requirements in order to avoid most retaliation claims. More often than not, an organization can prevent retaliation claims by adhering to the simple tenets discussed in this article. Further, in the event an organization is confronted with a frivolous retaliation lawsuit, adherence to these points will increase the likelihood of a swift, inexpensive, and successful result.

REFERENCES

Age Discrimination in Employment Act, Section 4(d), 29 U.S.C. § 623(d) (1967).

Americans with Disabilities Act, Section 503, 42 U.S.C. § 12203 (1990).

Breaux v. City of Garland, No. 3:94-CV–2291-D, U.S. District Court, Dallas, Texas (November 1997).

Casenas v. Fujisawa USA, Inc., 58 Cal. App. 4th 101 (1997).

Channon v. United Parcel Service, 629 N.W.2d 835 (Iowa, 2001).

Civil Rights Act of 1964, Title VII, Section 704(a), 42 U.S.C. § 2000e–3(a).

Clark Community School District v. Breeden, 532 U.S. 268 (2001).

Equal Employment Opportunity Commission. (1998). *Compliance Manual on Retaliation*, Section 8, p. 13. Retrieved May 30, 2005, from http://www.drlp.org/html/publications/EEOC/retaliation.html

Equal Pay Act. 29 U. S. C. 206(d) (1963).

Fair Employment and Housing Act. Cal. Govt. Code §§12900 *et seq.* (2005).

Foster v. Brown, 1998 U.S. Dist. LEXIS 4239 (N.D. Cal. 1998).

Hashimoto v. Dalton, 118 F.3d 671 (9th Cir. 1997).

Huff v. Boeing Co., 1997 U.S. App. LEXIS 30024 (9th Cir. 1997).

Mockler v. Multnomah County, 140 F.3d 808 (9th Cir. 1998). Retrieved on May 30, 2005, from http://caselaw.lp.findlaw.com/cgi-bin/getcase.pl?court=9th&navby=case&no=9635895

Ray v. Henderson, 217 F.3d 1234 (9th Cir. 2000).

Robinson v. Shell Oil Company, 519 U.S. 337 (1997).

Sarbanes–Oxley Act, 15 U.S.C. § 7201 *et. seq.* (2002).

Songco v. Century Quality Management, Inc., Superior Court, Los Angeles, CA (October 1997).

Travis-Barker v. U.S. Bank, NA, 1997 U.S. App. LEXIS 23922 (9th Cir. 1997).

Winarto v. Toshiba America Electric Components, 274 F.3d 1276 (9th Cir. 2001).

THE PSYCHOLOGIST-MANAGER JOURNAL, 2005, 8(2), 157–164

Human Resources Management Comes of Age in the Courtroom: California Formally Enshrines the Importance of Human Resources Expert Testimony for Employment Litigation

Jan C. Nielsen

Gwilliam, Ivary, Chioso, Cavalli & Brewer

This article provides some background on testimony about human resources management practices in the courtroom. The author, a plaintiff's counsel, contends that a milestone was reached recently when the California Court of Appeal expressly accepted such testimony as relevant subject matter in an employment-related civil case. Prior to that in California, oftentimes human resources experts were limited in testimony, or altogether excluded, because testimony about personnel matters was considered "junk science." The appellate court, however, also set some parameters on this type of expert testimony. The article provides further detail on some of the issues surrounding expert testimony in this field.

A milestone in the study of human resources (HR) management practices was reached recently but few so far have taken notice. On January 28, 2004, the days of industrial psychology or HR management being characterized as "junk science" in courtrooms abruptly ended with the California Court of Appeal's opinion, *Kotla v. Regents of the University of California* (2004). Now persons with such expertise formally join the ranks of recognized experts who clearly may testify in litigation.

Kotla was a horrendous employment case. On December 16, 1996, 48-year-old Lawrence Livermore National Laboratory employee, Dee Kotla, was giving testimony in a deposition in support of a sexual harassment plaintiff and former coworker. In effect, she testified against the Lab. During the deposition, the atmo-

Correspondence should be sent to Jan C. Nielsen, c/o Gwilliam, Ivary, Chiosso, Cavalli & Brewer, 1999 Harrison Street, Suite 1600, Oakland, CA 94612. E-mail: nielsen.jan@sbcglobal.net

sphere was so hostile that Kotla, who wasn't represented by an attorney, repeatedly protested she feared retaliation. One defense attorney insisted that she answer a question, saying: "You don't have anyone to tell you not to answer, so answer the question!" During the course of the testimony, the Lab's attorney demanded that Kotla reveal her work computer's password so the Lab could search her computer. Kotla refused. The attorney called her supervisor and described Kotla to him as a "hostile witness." The supervisor told Kotla to give the Lab's attorney her password.

A bathroom break was called. While Kotla occupied a stall in the women's restroom, she heard her employer's attorneys come in and talk out loud. The Lab's counsel said: "If Kotla knows what's good for her, she'll shut up."

Indeed, that very day the Lab's counsel accessed Kotla's computer, found some personal materials, including a very personal love letter to her friend and an Excel spreadsheet. The counsel called the University of California Police Department, and initiated a criminal investigation of Kotla for purportedly using her employer's computer to help out her lover's business. The police investigated Kotla for Penal Code violations relating to computer misuse. After the local district attorney declined to prosecute, the investigation was turned over to Kotla's management—just one day before the second installment for Kotla's deposition in the sex harassment case.

In the past, discipline for computer misuse at the Lab had been fairly minimal, mostly culminating in a brief suspension. Persons had been terminated in only two cases. A couple of scientists who had used the Lab's supercomputers to design a weapons system (under a personal contract with the Norwegian Navy) had been fired. An employee who ran a pornography server and downloaded gigabytes of pornography on a Lab computer had also been terminated.

By comparison, many misusers had hardly been disciplined at all. An employee who let his child play with an expensive top-line computer for 3 years, downloaded gigabytes of files, and blatantly attempted to impede the Lab's investigation of the misuse, had been docked 15 days pay. Employees who downloaded megabytes of pornography from the Internet had received 5-day suspensions. Someone who ran up $112 in personal phone calls had received only a written warning. In Kotla's case, the investigation found little evidence to support the charges (barely $4.30 in personal telephone calls and "insignificant" use of her computer to help her friend). Yet she was fired. Something was really "fishy" here. The termination occurred barely 1 month after Kotla had completed her deposition testimony. It was also brutal and abrupt, as if the message were "Get out of here, now, Dee!"

Kotla's psychological make-up was such that she suffered an extreme reaction to the Lab's action. That evening, February 20, 1997, she fell into a deep and severe depression. Kotla attempted suicide and nearly died.

The Lab had retaliated against Dee Kotla, and she nearly died as a result. At the trial, Lab witnesses contradicted one another, became angry on the stand, and the Lab's attorneys even argued that Kotla should thank them because after her breakdown she had gotten another job, and was now doing all right financially. The plaintiff's HR expert, a distinguished industrial psychologist, testified about how "generally accepted HR practices" had not been followed in the investigation and termination of Kotla. Additionally, the expert testified that various facts indicated that the Lab was motivated to retaliate and that the Lab had retaliated against Kotla. The defendant's HR officers testified that they did everything right. Matters they couldn't recall in deposition, suddenly, they were able to recall. The Lab did not bring its own HR expert because in deposition she had admitted that the Lab should have met with Kotla and tried to work things out before terminating her employment.

On March 11, 2002, after a 2-month trial, a majority of jurors found for Kotla under her complaint alleging retaliation and awarded her $1 million in total damages. The court later reduced that to $675,000 and awarded the plaintiff's attorneys fees, with a multiplier, for a total fees award of $1.4 million. In the end, the judgment added up to $2.1 million.

The Lab appealed. On January 28, 2004, in *Dee Kotla v. Regents of the University of California*, the Court of Appeals, First Appellate District, Division One reversed the award, and ordered a new trial, contending Kotla's HR expert's testimony was "improper and prejudicial." (The Regents manage the Laboratory under a contract with the United States Department of Energy.) But the Court of Appeal gave some as well as took away. In *Kotla*, the court expressly recognized the legitimacy of the testimony of HR experts in California courtrooms.

FOUNDATIONAL ELEMENTS OF HR EXPERT TESTIMONY: HR EXPERT TESTIMONY PRIOR TO KOTLA

In general, the admissibility of expert witness testimony in Federal and state courtrooms raises numerous issues, including, *inter alia,* is the opinion properly one for an expert? Is the expert qualified? Is the expert's opinion admissible? Often at the beginning of the trial the defense will submit a motion *in limine* or pre-trial motion requesting that the trial bar the expert from testifying on one of these grounds.

In assessing under the *in limine* motion whether the opinion is admissible, the court looks to whether the expert will improperly testify to a question of law, whether his opinion is based on conjecture, speculation, or matters not properly relied upon, and the expert's methodology. The United States Supreme Court has promulgated the Daubert test (*Daubert v. Merrell Dow Pharmaceuticals, Inc.,* 1993), whereby the court must assure that the expert is proposing to testify to (a) scientific knowledge that (b) will assist the trier of fact to understand or determine a fact in issue. "This entails," the Supreme Court explained in *Daubert*, "a preliminary assessment of whether the reasoning or methodology underlying the testimony is scientifically valid and of whether that reasoning or methodology can properly be applied" to the facts of the case. This entails an examination of whether the knowledge "can be tested," whether it can be "subjected to peer review," whether there is a "known or potential rate of error," and "whether there is wide-spread acceptance" (1993, par. c).

California follows a somewhat similar but in some respects markedly different rule, promulgated in *People v. Kelly* (1976). The *Kelly* Court declared that the admissibility of expert testimony that is based upon the application of a new scientific technique traditionally involves a two-step process: (a) the reliability of the method must be established and (b) the witness furnishing such testimony must be properly qualified as an expert. Additionally, quoting from *Frye v. United States* (1923), "the thing from which the deduction is made must be sufficiently established to have gained general acceptance in the particular field in which it belongs" (1923, at 1014). This test in California became known as the "*Kelly–Frye* test" for admissibility of expert witness testimony.

Daubert does not require a showing of "general acceptance" but "wide acceptance" is one of the factors considered under admissibility. Both *Daubert* and *Kelly–Frye* are conservative tests, conveying to trial courts faced with such admissibility issues an appropriate sense of caution. As such, these standards worked to limit substantially the testimony of experts. Judges, in general, had become hostile to expert witness testimony. In newer, less well-known fields such as HR, these factors weighed heavily against admissibility.

Prior to *Kotla*, although experts in the field of HR had testified in employment cases, the admissibility of such testimony varied from case to case. No case opinion formally established that HR expert testimony is relevant. There was little more than a hodgepodge of state and federal authorities whom a litigant could cite in support of allowing his HR expert to testify.

In *Colgan v. Fisher Scientific Co.* (1991), the Third Circuit held that the lower court erred in excluding a personnel expert's declaration that the employer had breached its standard procedures when it evaluated the plaintiff's performance. The court held that it was reasonable to infer that the untypical evaluation was the product of age discrimination.

In *Davis v. Combustion Engineering, Inc.* (1984), the Sixth Circuit held that the district court did not abuse its discretion in allowing a management professor to testify to his opinion, based on the employer's records, that the plaintiff was terminated because of his age. The expert testified that analysis of the employer's records had caused him to eliminate all other bases from the discharge.

In *Texas Department of Human Services v. Green* (1993), the Texas Court of Appeal affirmed a $13 million judgment ($3 million compensatory and $10 million punitive) in favor of an employee in a retaliatory firing case. The court held the trial court properly allowed two expert witnesses to express their opinions that the employer's cumulative acts constituted retaliation. The trial court also reasonably permitted one expert to testify about the importance of deterring retaliation against whistle blowers.

"JUNK SCIENCE"

Against this backdrop, in *Kotla* the Lab's attorney blustered in his brief to the California Court of Appeal that "junk science" had done in his client. The plaintiff's expert testimony in the field of industrial psychology or HR management, he insisted, was just plain "junk."

"When junk science masquerades as 'expert' testimony," he declared, "injustice is certain." Of course, HR expertise never was junk and could hardly be considered unjust, given a balanced look at employment litigation. Industrial psychology provides the scientific and empirical basis for HR management. It is a specialty field which is taught in colleges and universities and may lead to a master's or doctoral degree.

Indeed, HR has evolved its own standards of practice. Consultants regularly evaluate cases for employers, advise and assist in developing proper procedures and policies, assist in investigations, and regularly testify as experts in employment cases.

It is patently not unjust to have them testify. Employers have utilized their HR staff to look for ways to serve managers or to evade laws. Often, HR departments draft policies and procedures that assure employees fair and equitable treatment but don't follow them or fail to follow generally accepted practices in the HR field when terminating an employee. They usually have made the employee's termination "look good on paper," in a manner of speaking. In litigation, the employee-plaintiff not only has to tackle an employer with enormous resources and internal expertise but also must overcome a myriad of rules, policies, procedures, and practices–"on paper"–which allegedly sanitize the employer's actions vis-à-vis the employee.

In the past, without testimony from a person with specialized knowledge in HR, employment litigation plaintiffs were usually at a huge disadvantage in counteracting the testimony of the employers' HR personnel about the propriety of a termination. But for years, in pretrial motion after pretrial motion, defense attorneys fought to exclude or limit HR experts from testifying on behalf of plaintiffs in employment litigation. Often, especially given the hostile demeanor of courts to expert testimony in general, such testimony was excluded or at least substantially limited. Employers would then have witnesses from their own HR departments available to testify that nothing had been done wrong and everything had been done right according to their personnel policies and procedures.

KOTLA ESTABLISHES THAT HR EXPERTS CLEARLY MAY TESTIFY

Finally, on January 28, 2004, HR expert testimony became enshrined in California law, no longer to be derogatorily-labeled "junk science." In *Kotla*, the Court of Appeals specifically ruled that "Expert testimony on predicate issues within the expertise of a HR expert is clearly permissible" (115 Cal.App. 4th at 294). The Court cited examples of "predicate issues" that HR could appropriately testify about, including the assessment of "disproportionate punishment" and whether an employer "significantly deviated" from ordinary personnel procedures in taking retaliatory adverse employment action vis-à-vis the employee.

The Lab argued vociferously against admitting any HR testimony, because it was "on a subject well within the common experience of the jurors." In particular, it stated: "...[the] expertise, if any, was on a subject well within the common experience of the jurors. Where a question is 'resolvable by common knowledge,' there is no need for expert testimony ... If the jurors would be able to draw a conclusion from the facts testified to as easily and intelligently as the expert, the opinion testimony of the expert is not admissible" (115 Cal.App. 4th at 294–295 n. 6, 8).

Because the subject matter of *Kotla* involved the employer's retaliation against an employee, the Lab reminded the Court of Appeal that "most jurors either are employed or have been employed ... they are familiar with workplace discipline issues from ... everyday experience." The brief concluded that ordinary people are competent to assess human motivations, and that retaliation—*revenge*, in plain English—is a concept as old as humanity, one that jurors well understand.

"WORSE THAN JUNK SCIENCE"
ARGUMENTS BOOMERANG

The Lab had lost in the trial court, wanted to blame someone, and was angry with HR experts. Its brief went far beyond the "everyday experience of jurors" argument to denigrate altogether the field of industrial psychology as "not intellectually rigorous" and claimed it "was worse than 'junk science'—it was not even science at all" (115 Cal.App. 4th at 292).

In legal analysis and argument, lawyers and their clients often learn the hard way that going too far with arguments can cause them to boomerang. In the end, judges will reject the argument. Even worse, if the argument is too extreme the judges react negatively, and sometimes see fit to undercut the original advocating party's position. This happened with *Kotla*. The Court favored the Lab's position, felt that the plaintiff's expert had ventured too far with his opinions, and found error in the trial court's allowance of the expert's specific testimony relative to "indicators" or "retaliatory motive." It granted a new trial.

But the "worse than junk science" argument went too far, and the Court responded unfavorably. It implied that trial courts cannot limit or exclude HR expert testimony in litigation as junk or argue that it is not science at all, as they had done in the past. As set forth above, the *Kotla* Court agreed that HR management is "permissible" expert testimony.

The *Kotla* Court discounted these prior opinions and cited a number of federal opinions (*Barfield v. Orange County*, 1990; *Brink v. Union Carbide Corp.*, 1997; *Curtis v. Oklahoma City Public Schools Board*, 1998; *Lipsett v. University of*

Puerto Rico, 1990; *Smith v. Colorado Interstate Gas Co.*, 1992; *Ward v. Westland Plastics, Inc.*, 1980) that have heard "similar testimony in the employment context" and "rejected it." It seemed to have endorsed the view of the District Court in *Green v. Kinney Shoe Corp.* (D.D.C. 1988), which warned that expert testimony about an employer's motivations must be cautiously considered before it is admitted. But beyond testimony about motivations or testimony about indicators of illegal actions such as retaliation, *Kotla* appears to have opened the door so that the HR expert may testify about the full panoply of issues surrounding an employee's termination. Testimony simply has to be styled a certain way. For example, under *Kotla*, unless the expert has specific identical experience to rely upon, he cannot testify that a particular act or event in an employment case indicates retaliation against the employee. The expert lacks the foundation to testify in that manner. It appears he may however testify generally about the types of acts (or lack of them) that manifest retaliatory behaviors. Then, counsel can draw the linkage between the expert's testimony and the facts of the case in his closing argument to the jury. Further, if the defense, under its cross-examination of the expert, gets into the specific facts and the relationship of the case facts to HR practices, retaliation, or discrimination, then it may open the door even wider for the HR expert.

KNOW THE FACTS

One of the really glaring deficiencies, however, of the Court of Appeals opinion in *Kotla* is the way it overlooked the strong knowledge of facts that the plaintiff's HR expert had acquired in that case. Sometimes parties hire experts for show, pay them a bit of money for a cursory review, and have them testify. This *modus operandi* in employment cases can be disastrous. Any expert, particularly an expert on HR, must know the facts of the case extremely well. Gaining a clear understanding of the facts from reviewing depositions, motions, exhibits, and related testimony is part of a good expert's practice and essential to success on the stand. Absent such preparation, experts are seen as "hired guns," paid to advocate for the client, or usurping the attorney's role.

Additionally, time and again, because experts are expensive, the penny-wise party has failed to pay them sufficiently to review the case fully and become apprised of all details. In such cases the other party's attorney can usually pick them apart by showing that they were not aware of this or of that particular fact. The *Kotla* Court did not levy the usual criticism of "hired gun" at the plaintiff's expert, and couldn't, because he had been very well prepared and was thoroughly familiar with the facts. In one recent trial in Contra Costa County in which the author participated, the defendant's expert charged $500 per hr for her testimony and equally high fees for her review of the case. During her trial testimony, it was obvious that the party had limited its investment, because at the trial the expert did not have a good grasp of the facts. Incredibly, when cornered on the stand, she contended that for her to opine on the relevant issues, she didn't need to know the facts!

CONCLUSION: HR EXPERTS AFTER *KOTLA*

After *Kotla,* HR expert testimony on appropriate issues in employment cases will no longer be the object of derogatory "common knowledge" or "worse than junk science" references. It is a recognized field that may offer testimony which is helpful to a clearer understanding of issues surrounding employment litigation.

ACKNOWLEDGMENTS

Jan C. Nielsen is an attorney-at-law and experienced trial lawyer formerly with the law firm of Gwilliam, Ivary, Chiosso, Cavalli & Brewer in Oakland, California. He was one of the attorneys representing Dee Kotla. The expert witness was Jay Finkelman, Ph.D., who is the Editor of this Special Issue of *The Psychologist-Manager Journal.*

Uncited quotations in this article have been provided by the author.

POSTSCRIPT

Kotla v. Regents was retried in early 2005, with the same HR expert, and the plaintiff, Dee Kotla, won again. She received a judgement (including attorneys' fees) in the amount of $5.9 million.

REFERENCES

Barfield v. Orange County, 911 F.2d 644, 651 n. 8 (11th Cir. 1990).
Brink v. Union Carbide Corp., 41 F.Supp.2d 402, 405 (S.D.N.Y. 1997).
Colgan v. Fisher Scientific Co., 935 F.2d 1407 (3rd Cir. 1991) .
Curtis v. Oklahoma City Public Schools Bd., 147 F.3d 1200, 1219 (10th Cir. 1998).
Daubert v. Merrell Dow Pharmaceuticals, Inc., 509 U.S. 579 (1993).
Davis v. Combustion Engineering, Inc., 742 F.2d 916 (6th Cir. 1984).
Dee Kotla v. Regents of the University of California, (2004) 115 Cal.App. 4th 283.
Frye v. United States, 293 F. 1013, 1014 (D.C. Cir. 1923).
Green v. Kinney Shoe Corp., 704 F. Supp. 259, 260 (D.D.C. 1988).
Lipsett v. University of Puerto Rico, 740 F.Supp. 921, 925 (D.P.R. 1990).
People v. Kelly, 17 Cal.3d 24 (1976).
Smith v. Colorado Interstate Gas Co., 794 F.Supp. 1035, 1044 (D. Colo. 1992).
Texas Dept. of Human Services v. Green, 855 S.W.2d 136 (Tex. App. 1993).
Ward v. Westland Plastics, Inc., 651 F.2d 1266, 1270–1271 (9th Cir. 1980).

THE PSYCHOLOGIST-MANAGER JOURNAL, 2005, 8(2), 165–175
Copyright © 2005 by the Society of Psychologists in Management

Driving Distracted While In Your Employ: Liability Involving Cell Phones

Thomas H. Dinkelacker
Dimmich, Guldin, Dinkelacker & Brienza P. C.

This article provides an overview of potential liability to an employer arising out of employee cell phone use while operating a motor vehicle. It briefly describes cell phone technology and reviews in relevant part several prominent studies on the topic. Illustrated for comparison purposes are various statutes and legislative enactments or proposals addressing cell phone use in motor vehicles, as well as common law principles generally applicable to the same. Finally, considerations are identified to assist an employer in an analysis of the degree of risk imposed by employee cell phone use, a decision whether to implement a cell phone policy, and a determination of the content of any such policy.

It is a fact. Technology has expanded the geographical limit of the traditional workplace. Although business travel is not new, our ability to conduct business during travel is changing rapidly. Many suggest that the ability to communicate and exchange information during travel makes us more efficient but it also distracts us and potentially extends the employer's scope of liability for the actions of its employees.

This article does not concern itself with travel on planes and trains but rather automobiles. We drive faster on increasingly congested roadways with a hot coffee in one hand and electronic gadgetry in the other, conducting business along the way. The list of potential distractions is too lengthy to compile. This article focuses on the distractions created by technology and more particularly the cellular telephone. Other gadgets include computers, personal data assistants, CDs, DVDs, and those old stand-bys, the pen and pencil. Are we paying attention to the road and other, potentially distracted drivers?

Consider three scenarios, all of which began with cell phones and ended in court.

Correspondence should be sent to Thomas H. Dinkelacker, Esquire, Dimmich, Guldin, Dinkelacker & Brienza, P. C., 2970 Corporate Court, Suite 1, Orefield, PA 18069.

SCENARIO ONE

A stockbroker employed by a major brokerage firm drives into the city late on a Saturday afternoon for take-out at a local restaurant. He chooses the particular restaurant because he is soliciting the owner as a potential client and, while en route, he decides to make cold calls to prospective and current clients on his cell phone. When he reaches for the cell phone, the cord becomes entangled in the stick shift of his red Mercedes convertible and the phone slides out of his hand and on to the floor. He claims that he takes his eyes off of the road to pick up the phone and while doing so runs a red light. He strikes and kills a father of three who is on a motorcycle driving home from a convenience store where he has just picked up a package of hot dogs for the family dinner. The stockbroker flees the scene. Interestingly, the employee stockbroker claimed that everything he did, including attending church, benefited his employer because of the relationships created. Thus, in his opinion and that of the plaintiff, he was furthering the interests of his employer in virtually every activity of daily living (*Leroy G. Roberts v. Smith Barney, Inc., and James P. Tarone,* 1997).

SCENARIO TWO

A manufacturing company employs over-the-road truck drivers to deliver concrete materials. To enhance communication with the plant, the truck is equipped with a cell phone provided by the employer. In addition, the employer has a policy for cell phone use providing only for company use and requiring among other things that the driver pull off the road when the phone rings, bring the vehicle to a stop and only then return the telephone call. In this case, the phone rings, the driver knows who is calling, and the driver dutifully pulls off the road; however, the secondary road does not permit him to pull all the way off, and another driver rear-ends the stopped truck and is injured (*Tielle v. Keystone Concrete Block and Supply Company,* 2001).

SCENARIO THREE

An attorney with a metropolitan law firm is driving home from a business meeting at approximately 10 p.m., making cell phone calls along the way. It is later alleged that she is driving erratically and with great negligence, moving out of her lane and onto the shoulder, and it is further alleged that another driver is actually run off the road. Allegedly, the attorney made as many as eight phone calls and billed the time for those calls to firm clients, thus benefiting the employer. Tragically, after passing a vehicle parked on the shoulder, the attorney strikes a pedestrian. She does not stop. The victim's spouse and a police officer find the victim with a pulse but cannot resuscitate her and the young mother is pronounced dead at the hospital (*Young Ki Yoon, Personal Representative of Naeun Yoon, Deceased v. Jane L. Wagner,* 2001).

In each scenario the employer was sued civilly for negligence. In Scenarios One and Three, the employee was sued and subjected to criminal proceedings for leaving the scene of the accident. In Scenario One, the employer did not have a cell phone policy; however in Scenario Two there was such a policy and, indeed, it was arguable that the policy contributed to the accident. The cases of the stockbroker and attorney illustrate problems inherent in the expansion of the traditional workplace.

Are the above-cited claims unusual? To answer that question fairly, one need ask only a simple follow-up question: Can any of us claim that we have never been distracted by cell phones and other pieces of office technology that find their way into our automobiles? Because for many that answer is an unequivocal "no," we must give considerable thought to the dramatic increase in the exposure of employers to lawsuits and other claims facilitated by the doctrine of *respondeat superior.* This is Latin for "let the master answer," a doctrine of the common law that creates liability in the employer for the negligent or wrongful acts of the employee who is acting in furtherance of the employer's interests (Black's Law Dictionary, 1968).

This article attempts to raise issues and awareness concerning that risk. Studies of cell phone usage while driving are discussed and the law is briefly reviewed. Cellular calls do not respect state lines; we are a country of at least 52 separate jurisdictions, many of which are attempting to address distracted driving and cell phone use. It is beyond the scope of this article to discuss the myriad of federal, state, and common law concepts that address the liability of an employer for the acts of an employee. Any such liability is dependant upon the common and statutory law in effect in the jurisdiction and the particular facts of each case. Finally, this article examines considerations with respect to employer cell phone policies.

CELLULAR TECHNOLOGY

The cell phone has been described as an "extremely sophisticated radio" which operates in connection with a system of "cells" (Brian & Tyson, 2001). A cell covers about 10 square miles and forms part of a grid system. Each cell contains a tower and radio equipment and, as the user travels between cells, the signal is transferred to the next cell. If the voice channel is not recognized, or if no channel is available, the signal may be dropped. Not all frequency areas overlap and not all are adjacent to one another. Accordingly, the cell phone signal may be affected when a "dead zone" is reached. Moreover, terrain will affect signal strength.

Cell phones and their providers offer numerous options and services. These can include sending and receiving e-mail, text messaging, appointment information, voice mail, and access to informational services, including the stock market. The wide array of services increases the opportunities for distraction, and some of the services and features may relate directly to the employee's performance of his or her job.

STUDIES OF CELL PHONE USE AND ACCIDENTS

To determine whether a policy for cell phone use is appropriate (and, if so, the elements of that policy) one must consider the findings of the many studies performed in recent years concerning the relationship between cell phone use and automobile accidents and the specific tasks associated with cell phone use which contribute to accidents. Studies have been performed by various states, the National Highway Transportation Safety Administration (NHTSA), independent researchers, and other organizations (Joint State Government Commission, 2001; NHTSA, 1997; Redelmeier & Tibshirani, 1997).

One study (Redelmeier & Tibshirani, 1997) set forth a number of interesting findings. The researchers studied 699 drivers with cell phones who were involved in motor vehicle collisions resulting in substantial property damage but no personal injury. Each individual's cell phone calls on the day of the collision and during the previous week were analyzed through the use of detailed billing records. Over 26,000 cell phone calls were made during the 14-month study period. Redelmeier and Tibshirani found that the relative risk of a collision was consistent among individuals despite different personal characteristics. Specifically, although younger drivers had a higher relative risk of an accident when using a cell phone than older drivers, that increase was not significant, and increased risk applied even to individuals with many years of experience in the use of cell phones. The highest relative risk was found among drivers who had not graduated from high school. In no group of individuals was cell phone use associated with reduced risk and, most interestingly, hands-free devices did not appear to result in safer driving than hand-held counterparts.

Redelmeier and Tibshirani made a number of important observations:

1. Use of cell phones while driving was associated with a quadrupling of the risk of a collision (similar to the hazard associated with a blood alcohol level of the legal limit).
2. Cell phones were beneficial as they allowed drivers to make emergency calls quickly.
3. Generally, cell phone calls were short and infrequent, leading the researchers to explain the absence of a marked increase in overall collisions.

No safety advantage was observed with respect to hands-free devices as compared to the use of hand-held devices, leading to the possible explanation that accidents result from inattention rather than dexterity. The authors cautioned against interpreting the data to show that cell phones were harmful and that their use should be restricted. They pointed out that even if a causal relationship between cell phones and accidents were established, drivers were vulnerable to other distractions that could offset any potential reduction in the risks associated with restricting the use of cell phones.

A more recent study (Cohen & Graham, 2003) estimated that the use of cell phones by drivers may result in approximately 2,600 deaths, 330,000 injuries, and 1.5 million instances of property damage in America each year. Fatalities were estimated as ranging between 800 and 8,000 per year.

In November 1997, the NHTSA issued a report entitled *An Investigation of the Safety Implications of Wireless Communication in Vehicles*. In the report summary, NHTSA noted that trends in technology and society, combined with a desire to work on the road, resulted in a move towards integration of technologies such that cell phones were the focal point of a mobile office. NHTSA stated

> It was inevitable that the reduced size, reduced cost and increased functionality of the cellular telephone would find its use by drivers in vehicles increasing dramatically. Indeed, time spent commuting, caught up in traffic and just plain traveling could now be productive. (Introduction, paragraph 3)

Addressing crash data, NHSTA noted that "phone conversation rather than dialing" was the most frequently cited pre-crash occurrence, and that

> Contrary to expectations, the majority of drivers were talking on their telephones rather than dialing at the time of the crash. A few drivers also were startled when their cellular telephones rang, and as they reached for their phones, they ran off the road ... The overwhelming majority of cell phone users were in the striking vehicle, and struck cars or other large objects that were in clear view of the driver. (Crash Data, paragraph 4)

The studies suggest that a number of activities have an impact, although to varying degrees, on a driver's attention. These include distractions associated with the handling and operation of the cell phone and the distraction of conversation. Indeed, it is suggested that distractions associated with complex conversation have a greater impact than the distractions associated with the handling and operation of the cell phone itself. Therefore, any cell phone policy which focuses solely on the use of hands-free devices is probably flawed. Although conversation often occurs in a vehicle, the availability of the cell phone allows a lone occupant to engage in conversation, and driving alone may prompt a desire to make that time productive.

STATUTORY AND COMMON LAW

The phrase *very few* adequately summarizes the number of jurisdictions which have addressed cell phone use through legislation. New Jersey prohibits the holders of driver examination permits from using a cell phone or other wireless communication device. The term *use* includes talking, listening, or using the keys. In New York, a person may not operate a motor vehicle while using a hand-held mobile phone and, in Tennessee, computers or other electronic displays in utility vehicles may be used only while the vehicle is stopped, standing, or parked. Finally, in Rhode Island, Pennsylvania and Utah, cell phone use is prohibited by school bus drivers. Several states have enacted laws requiring studies of the relationship between cell phone use and automobile accidents, including New Jersey, Virginia, Delaware, and Florida. In Rhode Island, the Governor vetoed a law prohibiting the use of hand-held mobile phones while operating a bicycle or motor vehicle (National Conference of State Legislatures, 2004; NHTSA, 2004).

Several states have legislation which is pending on an active or inactive basis. For example, approximately nine states including California, Delaware, and Illinois had legislation pending in 2003 prohibiting the use of hand-held phones while driving. Similarly, approximately 11 states, including California, Illinois, New York, Maryland, and Michigan, had legislation pending to regulate cell phone use based upon the age or status of the operator. For example, California was considering legislation which would prohibit drivers under the age of 18 from using a cell phone while driving. Illinois and Maryland were considering prohibiting such use by individuals holding an instruction license. Finally, five states including Indiana, Maryland, Mississippi, New York, and Wyoming were considering a prohibition on the use of cell phones. In most instances, the proposed legislation included exceptions for emergencies. In addition, many states were considering enhanced penalties for cell phone use and other, general legislation concerning inattentive driving. An excellent resource for investigating the status of cell phone legislation throughout the United States is the NHTSA Legislative Tracking Database (2004).

It is important not to assume that the absence of specific legislation concerning cell phone use renders such activity beyond the realm of law enforcement. To the contrary, most if not all states have legislation concerning inattentive or reckless driving. Some of the difficulties in gaining passage of cell phone legislation appear to include the view that cell phone use is only one of many behaviors associated with inattentive driving, the lack of a clear causal connection between cell phones and a significant increase in the risk of accidents, the existence of inattentive driving statutes already on the books, and a recognition that the cell phone has a positive impact in emergency situations.

In 2003, New Jersey Senator Jon Corzine proposed legislation to prohibit the use of hand-held phones by motor vehicle operators. This legislation, known as SB179, would require states to enact hand-held phone laws or risk losing 5% of their federal transportation funding for the 1st year violation and 10% in subsequent years (National Conference of State Legislatures, 2004).

Although a violation of the statutory law may give rise to *negligence per se* (that is, the violation of a statute or ordinance is proof of negligence provided that a causal relationship exists between the statutory violation and the occurrence; Black's Law Dictionary, 1968), one must also consider the common law. As noted previously, the doctrine of *respondeat superior* renders the employer liable for the negligent acts of the employee performed in the course and scope of the employment; and although there is typically little dispute as to whether an individual is an employee, the question of whether the employee is acting in the course and scope of his employment is a different situation. Of course, that question can only be answered on a fact-by-fact basis applying the law of the relevant jurisdiction. However, some general authorities can be cited in this regard.

The *Restatement of Agency* is a series of treatises concerning specific areas of the law and is prepared under the auspices of the American Law Institute (ALI, 1958). These treatises reflect the scholarly thought of experts in various legal fields concerning the social function of the particular branch of the law. The treatises do not necessarily reflect the law in any jurisdiction but the courts often favorably cite them as an accurate description of the law of those jurisdictions. Section 228 of the *Restatement (Second) of Agency* describes that conduct which places an employee within the scope of employment to include conduct which is of the kind that the person is employed to perform, which occurs substantially within the authorized time and space limits of the employment, and which is actuated at least in part by a purpose to serve the employer. This section provides further that conduct of an employee is not within the scope of employment if it is different in kind from that authorized, far beyond the authorized time or space limits, or too little actuated by a purpose to serve the employer.

Section 239 of the *Restatement (Second) of Agency* should also be considered. This section addresses the use of instrumentalities by an employee and provides that an employer is not liable for injuries caused by the employee's negligent use of an instrumentality if the instrumentality is substantially different in kind from that authorized as a means of performing the employer's service or if it is understood that the employer has no right to control the use of the instrumentality. Of course the instrumentality at issue includes the cell phone and quite possibly the automobile.

Returning to the scenarios presented earlier, in the case of the concrete delivery truck, the use of the cell phone was consistent with the employment, and in fact the cell phone was provided by the employer. With respect to the stockbroker, the question arose as to whether traveling for take-out food at a local restaurant on a Saturday night placed him within the times and spaces authorized for his employment (*Leroy G. Roberts v. Smith Barney, Inc., and James P. Tarone*, 1997). Clearly, business could not be transacted on a Saturday night and picking up take-out food (even from a client or prospective client) seemed to have little relationship to the employment. However, in the case of the attorney, traveling home from an evening meeting and making billable telephone calls might be deemed to fall within the parameters of *Restatement* Sections 228 and 239.

Although not providing definitive answers, and not necessarily representing the law of any particular jurisdiction, the *Restatement (Second) of Agency* (ALI, 1958) illustrates the fact-specific analysis which must occur with respect to litigation arising out of an accident occasioned by the use of a cell phone and an automobile.

CELL PHONE POLICIES

Before addressing the need for and content of a cell phone policy, one should first consider facts which may be used in the course of litigation to support or refute the applicability of the doctrine of *respondeat superior*. A nonexclusive list of considerations includes:

1. Whether the employer owns the cell phone or reimburses expenses for the cell phone.
2. Whether the employer owns the vehicle or reimburses travel or vehicular expenses.
3. Whether the employer knows which, if any, employees have or use cell phones in the conduct of business.
4. Whether the employer provides all materials and information necessary for the employee to perform his or her work at the office.
5. Whether the employee is paid during his or her time while on the cell phone or whether the client is billed for the employee's time while on the cell phone.
6. Whether the employer's business can be transacted over the cell phone.
7. Whether ownership or access to a cell phone or a vehicle is a prerequisite to the employment or part of the job description.
8. Whether representations were made by the employer to the employee during the job interview concerning the necessity or benefits of a cell phone.
9. Whether use of the cell phone is a convenience to the employee.
10. Whether the employer has a cell phone or automobile policy.

Although this is not an exhaustive list, considering the previous material should assist an employer in determining and assessing the degree of risk posed by the employee's use of a cell phone and vehicle and whether a cell phone policy is appropriate. One should keep in mind that having a cell phone policy and not enforcing it may lead to allegations of direct liability of the employer (as opposed to just *respondeat superior*) should an accident occur. Conversely, having a cell phone policy (when one is not needed) could support allegations that an employee is in the course and scope of employment while on the phone when in fact he or she is not.

For an employer to determine whether a cell phone policy should be established, the following considerations are helpful:

1. What is the business of the employer and is it primarily conducted from an office setting?
2. Do clients travel to the office to conduct or consummate business or do employees travel to the clients?
3. Does the employer provide an automobile or reimburse automobile or automobile travel-related expenses?
4. Does the employer provide a cell phone or reimburse cell phone-related expenses incurred by the employee?
5. Does the employer provide all materials or equipment necessary to conduct the work at the office?
6. What efficiencies, if any, are gained through cell phone use?
7. Do employees need cell phones to adequately perform the work or are they simply a matter of convenience for the employee?
8. Does the substance of the employee's work require that he or she travel by automobile and maintain contact with the office or the clientele?
9. Are employees being paid for time on the cell phone or are clients being billed for such time?

If, after analyzing the need for a cell phone policy it is determined that one is appropriate, one must consider the contents of that policy. In this regard, common sense reigns supreme. Some practical recommendations include

1. Review the principal scientific studies and their findings concerning the nature of the distractions caused by cell phones and the demographics of high-risk individuals.
2. Consider the nature of the distractions in the context of the use to which the employee will put the cell phone (i.e., will the calls be lengthy and complex or short and directional, keeping in mind that studies suggest that the primary distraction is the conversation and not cell phone operation).
3. Be specific as to the procedures for cell phone use, including where, when, and how the cell phones should be used.
4. Establish a time window in which it is considered that the employee will be in the scope of employment. (Is the stockbroker really serving the interests of his employer by attending church services or patronizing a local restaurant?)
5. Consider whether use of the cell phone should be prohibited at certain times and in the course of certain activities (such as commuting to and from

work, an activity which has traditionally been considered not work-related).

6. Make the cell phone policy mandatory and establish it as a positive and specific work order (use words such as *shall* and *will* to describe the activities expected of employees).

7. Establish who is responsible for the payment or reimbursement of costs and under what circumstances.

8. Consider the role of the cell phone in emergency situations and provide a clear definition of what constitutes an emergency (remember that not all states have "Good Samaritan" laws).

9. Consider requiring the use of safer technologies such as hands-free devices.

10. Know the status and content of the cell phone laws in your jurisdiction and the surrounding jurisdictions in which your employees may travel.

11. Regardless of the existence of specific cell phone laws, understand the common law of the jurisdiction in which the employees work and under what circumstances the employee is considered to be in the course and scope of employment.

12. Understand that the potential expansion of the work place could affect the employer's worker's compensation exposure in addition to general liability. For example, under the "coming and going" rule, an employee's commute to and from work is not considered work-related. However, if the employee is engaged in an accident while using the cell phone during the commute, is he or she entitled to worker's compensation benefits?

CONCLUSION

Having a clearly defined cell phone policy will help defend against a claim of *respondeat superior*, when appropriate, and this is an incentive to create a thoughtful policy. Of course, the ultimate consideration is safety, and the best way to avoid the lawsuit is to avoid the accident.

REFERENCES

American Law Institute. (1958). *Restatement of the law second, agency.* St. Paul, MN: American Law Institute Publishers.

Black, H. C. (1968). *Black's Law Dictionary* (Rev. 4th Ed.) St. Paul Minn: West Publishing Co.

Cohen, J. T., & Graham, J. D. (2003). A revised economic analysis of restrictions on the use of cell phones while driving. *Risk Analysis, 23,* 5–17.

Brian, M., & Tyson, J. (2001) *"How Cell Phones Work."* Retrieved March 29, 2004, from http://www.howstuffworks.com

Joint State Government Commission, General Assembly of the Commonwealth of Pennsylvania. (2001, December). *Driver distractions and traffic safety.* Staff report pursuant to 2000 Senate Resolution No. 127.

Leroy G. Roberts, Administrator of the Estate of Michael L. Roberts v. Smith Barney, Inc., and James P. Tarone, No. 97-CV–2727 (E.D. PA, 1997).

National Conference of State Legislatures. (2004, January 23) Retrieved February 25, 2004, from: http://www.ncsl.org

National Highway Traffic Safety Administration. (1997). *An investigation of the safety implications of wireless communications in vehicles.* Retrieved on June 12, 2005, from http://www/nhtsa.dot.gov./people/injury/research/wireless/

National Highway Traffic Safety Administration (2004). *Legislative tracking database.* Retrieved on February 23, 2004, from http://www.ntsa.dot.gov.ncsl/Index.dfm

Redelmeier, D. A., & Tibshirani, R. J. (1997). Association between cell-telephone calls and motor vehicle collisions. *New England Journal of Medicine, 336*(7), 453–458.

Tielle v. Keystone Concrete Block and Supply Company, No. 2001-CV–3396 (Lackawanna County, PA, 2001).

Young Ki Yoon, Personal Representative of Naeun Yoon, Deceased v. Jane L. Wagner, et al., C.L 24892 (Loudoun County, Virginia, 2001).

THE PSYCHOLOGIST-MANAGER JOURNAL, 2005, 8(2), 177–187

Computer and Internet Use in the Work Place: A Common Sense Approach

Gene D. Vorobyov

LaMore, Brazier, Riddle & Giampaoli

This article provides an overview of key legal issues arising out of computer and Internet use in the workplace. It surveys federal and state laws regulating each of these issues. This article also includes various suggested strategies for employers to deal with these issues. These suggested strategies are based on an analysis of the applicable laws, academic legal treatises, and the respective needs of employers and employees. The goal of this article is to help employers deal with the legal challenges arising out of computer and Internet use in the work place without losing good will and loyalty of their employees.

Computer use in the American workplace has become both commonplace and a commercial necessity. But along with all the commercial advantages computer and Internet use bring to employers, they also present a number of difficult challenges. For example, can an employer do anything about an employee who seems much more interested in plotting his or her next move in *Civilization III: Conquests* than in returning the clients' phone calls? Sid Meier's *Civilization III: Conquests* is the latest and the best in the series of historical, political, and military strategy computer games in the *Civilization* series created by Atari. This game is a must-buy for anyone interested in history or politics but it has been known to slow down office productivity to a barely detectible crawl. What about an employee who is passing jokes that would make *News Radio's* Phil Hartman blush? Can anything be done to prevent disclosure of these inappropriate e-mail communications when one of the more sensitive e-mail communication recipients decides to file a lawsuit against the company for creating a stressful or discriminatory work environment? And, more importantly, how does an employer address these challenges while maintaining a sane and productive workplace that does not resemble NBC's *Working*? (This

---

Correspondence should be sent to Gene D. Vorobyov, 795 Burnett Avenue, Apt. 10, San Francisco, CA 94131. E-mail: gvorobyov@lbrg.com

show is a 1997 sitcom in which Matt plays a college graduate trying to find his way around a grotesquely bizarre and hostile corporation.)

As one might expect, in the last 20 years the legal system has been about a step behind in addressing these problems. Nevertheless, existing federal and state privacy laws and recent federal and state court decisions still give distressed employers some options in addressing these challenges. The purpose of this article is to present some of the major challenges faced by employers when it comes to employee use of the employer's computers and to suggest legal and practical methods for dealing with these challenges.

MONITORING E-MAIL COMMUNICATION AND INTERNET USE

Applicable Laws

Many employees might be surprised to find out that despite several federal and state privacy protection laws, their employers generally have a legal right to monitor employee e-mail communication and Internet use. However, before employers rush to intercept, monitor, or search each and every employee communication or online activity, they need to understand the nature of the applicable privacy laws that limit such monitoring efforts.

Federal law. First, employers (and their in-house counsel) should become familiar with the federal Electronic Communications Privacy Act of 1986 (ECPA). Many state privacy laws are modeled after ECPA. Although this statute was enacted in response to the Watergate scandal before the explosion in the computer and Internet use, the statute was wisely made directly applicable to then-emerging electronic communication technology. As a general rule, ECPA prohibits interception, disclosure, use, or unauthorized access of most electronic communications, including e-mail communication. ECPA (1986) does provide several key exceptions:

1. If an employer provides a system for electronic communication, it may lawfully intercept any electronic communication sent within that system in the ordinary course of the employer's business or to protect the employer's property rights.

2. An employer can lawfully intercept an electronic communication if it is a party to that communication or if one of the parties to that communication gives its consent.

3. If an employer provides a system for electronic communication, it can access stored communications on that system as necessary in the ordinary course of employer's business or to protect the employer's property.

Employers should not assume that the "ordinary course of business" exception provides an open-ended interception or monitoring license. ECPA only permits employers to intercept a communication to determine if it is business-related (Sidbury, 2001). Once the nature of the communication is determined, ECPA does not permit employers to engage in further monitoring. Also, ECPA does not permit employers to intercept personal e-mail communications under the "ordinary course of business" exception. More importantly, it is clear that employers cannot intercept employee e-mail communications (business or personal) without notice to employee. Finally, although this issue has not been settled by the courts, employers are required to give notice to employee before monitoring employee's stored e-mail communication.

Federal Constitution.   Public employers also need to be aware of the constitutional implications of the privacy provisions of the federal Constitution on their right to search a computer used by an employee at work. Neither federal nor state Constitutions have any bearing on private employers (*Burton v. Wilmington Parking Authority*, 1961).

U.S. Constitution does not contain a specific amendment creating individual right to privacy. However, the Fourth Amendment of the U.S. Constitution prohibits the government from conducting unreasonable searches and seizures. To establish that a search conducted by the employer violated the employee's Fourth Amendment rights, an employee needs to establish (a) that the employer searched a place in which an employee had a subjective expectation of privacy and (b) that the expectation of privacy was one the society was prepared to recognize as reasonable (*California v. Ciraolo*, 1986; *Katz v. United States*, 1967). In *Katz*, the Court noted that the determination that one's privacy interests are protected requires a subjective expectation of privacy which the society is willing to recognize as reasonable. It should be noted that in recognizing an employee's objective and subjective expectation of privacy at work, the U.S. Supreme Court in *O'Connor v. Ortega* (1987) noted that such expectation of privacy was more diminished than the one the employee would have at home. As a result, unlike law enforcement officials, a public employer conducting a legitimate non-investigatory work-related search of an employee's work area does not need to obtain a search warrant or have probable cause to conduct such a search.

Nevertheless, such a search must comply with the standard of reasonableness to be constitutional. The *O'Connor* court also provided guidance, albeit in very general terms, regarding the scope of a work-related search. To be reasonable under the federal Constitution, an employer's search (a) must be justified at its inception and (b) must be reasonably related in scope to the circumstances that justified the search in the first place.

It is well settled that an employee whose Fourth Amendment rights have been violated by a search may sue his or her employer for money damages. However, in the last decade, federal courts have not been very receptive to public employee lawsuits alleging that employer searches of their work computers resulted in Fourth Amendment violation. For example, *Bohach v. City of Reno* (1996) held that police officers had no reasonable expectation of privacy in e-mail communication messages sent through their public employer's computer system.

Furthermore, in *Clark v. Regents of University of California* (1997), the defendant received tips that some of its employees had accepted kickbacks and misused the defendant's property for personal use. In response to these tips, the defendant performed an audit of the plaintiff's department at the University and asked the plaintiff to return a surplus computer to the defendant. The plaintiff asked the defendant's permission to delete some personal files first. When the defendant refused permission to delete and searched the computer in question, it found sexually explicit materials. The plaintiff filed a federal lawsuit against the defendant alleging that the search was unconstitutional but the court rejected the lawsuit and found the search reasonable. The court concluded that bacuase the employer already had some evidence that the plaintiff's department was engaged in taking kickbacks and misusing property, it had a right to investigate whether the plaintiff engaged in that behavior. Plaintiff's request to delete personal files only increased the defendant's reasonable suspicion and further justified the search. The court also concluded that the limited nature of the search, that is, retrieval of the plaintiff's files from the defendant's computer, was consistent with the purpose of the search and thus reasonable.

A particularly important lesson to draw from *Clark* is that employers need very little evidence to establish reasonableness of their searches. In *Clark*, the court upheld the search despite the fact that it had no evidence (or even a reason to suspect) that the plaintiff himself engaged in inappropriate behavior (at least until the plaintiff made an incriminating request to delete files). The court explained that although lack of particularized suspicion might invalidate a search that requires probable cause, such particularized suspicion is not required for a work-place search based only on reasonableness.

State constitutions.   Unlike the federal Constitution, some state constitutions have expressly created an individual right to privacy. Ten state constitutions expressly guarantee a citizen's right to privacy: Alaska, Arizona, California, Florida, Hawaii, Illinois, Louisiana, Montana, South Carolina, and Washington.

Despite the express constitutional guarantees, state courts appear to be just as unsympathetic as federal courts to employees' claims that employer search of their work computers violates their state constitutional right to privacy. For example, in *TBG Insurance Services Corp. v. Superior Court* (2002), in a strongly worded opinion, the court refused to recognize an employee's subjective expectation of privacy as reasonable when the employee agreed in writing that his employer could monitor his computer use.

State common law claims.   Because private employees have no right to bring Fourth Amendment claims against their employers, some employees have turned to state law causes of action for invasion of privacy (Sidbury, 2001). To prevail on such a claim, the plaintiff would have to show that the employer's search of his or her computer (a) was highly offensive to a reasonable person and (b) that the plaintiff had a reasonable expectation of privacy. But courts of different states have unanimously rejected such claims, reasoning that employees do not have a reasonable expectation of privacy in the employer's computer.

Suggested Approaches

In light of the state and federal privacy laws discussed earlier, the challenge for any employer is to find a way to make sure employees are not misusing employer's computer system without resorting to "Big Brother" tactics that would likely lower office morale to unproductive levels (Li, n.d.). One of the most effective ways to deal with the issue of monitoring computer and Internet use is a company-wide policy regarding computer and Internet use.

From a legal standpoint, a well drafted computer and Internet use policy would provide the notice required by ECPA before transmitted or stored e-mail communication or Web hits could be intercepted or monitored. A clear and explicit policy regarding computer use would also serve to lessen employee expectation of privacy in the work computer and thus defeat any lawsuits based on the violation of the constitutional right to privacy.

From a management standpoint, a good policy would not only protect employer's property and prevent liability from employee misuse of computers but it would also explain the reasons for enacting the policy and the goals the policy strives to achieve. This is the employer's chance to make it clear to the employees that its objective is not to monitor their every movement throughout the working day but to ensure that the company functions well and remains financially healthy. After all, all employees have a direct stake in the continuing financial health of the employer and they should be aware of situations in which their misuse of computers and Internet could jeopardize the company.

As to the major issues to be covered by the policy, here is the list of such issues:

1. Whether the company's e-mail communication system can be used for personal messages.

2. Whether any company information can be sent to an e-mail communication address outside the company.

3. Whether and to what extent the company will monitor contents of e-mail communication. This portion of the policy should include an explanation of the employer's and employees' respective legal rights regarding access and use of the computer system and the Internet.

4. Whether employees are allowed to send encrypted e-mail communication messages.

5. What types of files or images are prohibited from being sent using the computer system.

6. The policy should make it perfectly clear that e-mail communications that discriminate based on other's race, national origin, gender, sexual orientation, age, religious, or political beliefs will not be tolerated and could lead to disciplinary actions or dismissal.

7. The policy should outline procedures for disciplining employees in violation of the policy. Public employers should be aware of the due process protections they may have to provide to their employees and these rights should be specified in the policy. Even private employers should consider giving employees at least a modicum of procedural due process before imposing discipline or termination for violation of the policy.

There may still be other issues. Employers should work closely with their in-house counsel in developing and enforcing the policy in order to make sure that it meets the employer's goals.

Once such policy is drafted, the employer should distribute it to all employees and ask them to review and sign the acknowledgment that employees understand the policy and agree to be bound by it. Individual employee consent to such policy may even be made a condition of employment. The courts have held that such individual employee consent is valid even if it is a precondition to employment (*TBG Insurance Services Corp. v. Superior Court*, 2002).

A word of caution to employers is necessary. Just because an employer might legally be entitled to monitor e-mail communication and Internet use does not necessarily mean that such indiscriminate monitoring is a good idea from a management standpoint. As employers continue to demand longer hours from their employees, employers have to expect that employees will have to conduct at least some of their personal business at work. It is not a good idea for the employers to engage in monitoring of such personal communications, particularly if these communications do not affect employee productivity.

Also, claiming an unlimited right to monitor all communications, particularly as a condition of employment, could create employee morale problems from the start. It should also be noted that reliance on consent obtained as a condition of employment is dangerous because a court might conclude that employee consent was coerced.

Therefore, employers should consider a proposal by U.S. District Judge James M. Rosenbaum voluntarily to restrict *carte blanche* searches of employees. Judge Rosenbaum (2001) proposes private employers consider injecting a modicum of procedural due process in employee searches; most public employers are legally obligated to do so. Judge Rosenbaum proposed a so-called "cyber time-out," which would consist of employer giving an employee *short* advance notice of the impending search, which would include a description of the area to be searched. During that notice period, an employee should not be allowed to delete anything from the computer, but should have some opportunity to try to resolve employer's concerns that prompted the search in the first place or to utilize legal remedies to challenge the upcoming search.

Finally, one additional way employers can lower employee reasonable expectation of privacy is to issue passwords to employees and to require employees to reveal the selected password to the employer. To alleviate any employee concerns about unlimited monitoring of personal e-mail communication, an employer might think about a provision in the computer and Internet use policy that would specify the conditions under which employers could use that password to gain access to employees' computers.

In the alternative, employers do not have to require employees to reveal their personally selected password but should retain an ability to override that password, as necessary. The computer and Internet use policy should clearly advise employees of the employer's ability and intent to do so, as necessary.

Workplace Computer Use and Litigation

Antidiscrimination lawsuits.   Employers face a real danger of being a target of an antidiscrimination lawsuit based on employees' inappropriate computer or Internet use. Such liability could be and actually has been alleged when an employee uses the company e-mail communication system to send racial jokes. For example, in *Owens v. Morgan Stanley & Co.* (1997), two African-American employees sued Morgan Stanley for racial discrimination. One of the allegations included a charge that a white employee authored and sent an e-mail communication containing a racist joke through Morgan Stanley's computer system. Although the court concluded that a single e-mail communication does not create a hostile work environment, it did not say that racist or sexist e-mail communication could never amount to a hostile work environment prohibited by federal antidiscrimination statutes.

Similar danger exists in situations where employees send, download, or print sexually explicit materials in the work place, particularly in the areas where these materials could be seen by other employees. A careless employer that allows its computer system to create a hostile work environment could be held liable for failure to prevent creation of such an environment. For example, in *Sheffield v. Department of Social Services County of Los Angeles*, 2003, the court held that a public employer had a duty to prevent harassment and to take reasonable steps to protect the harassed employee once it became aware of the harassment allegations. One California court has already used evidence of e-mails generated on the employer's computer to find that the employer may have created a hostile working environment. *Costic v. Trammell Crow Co.* (2003) held that hostile work environment in violation of the California Fair Employment and Housing Act was created in part by allowing employees to send e-mail communications with dirty jokes about the plaintiff.

Once again, the most effective tools at the employer's disposal are well-drafted workplace and computer use policies. These policies should be distributed to each and every employee. Employers should require all employees to sign an acknowledgment that they have read and understood the policies.

In the general workplace policy, an employer should advise employees that defamation, harassment, or discrimination on any basis, or creation of hostile work environment on any basis, will not be tolerated. This policy should also create a mechanism for any aggrieved employee to bring allegations of harassment or hostile workplace environment to the employer's attention. The policy should also establish a process for investigation of such complaints and resulting disciplinary measures, with at least a modicum of due process for the complainant and the alleged perpetrator.

In the computer use policy, the employer should reiterate the antidiscrimination, antiharassment, and antidefamation prohibition and warn employees that any use of the employer's computer to perpetrate such conduct is a violation of the policy that would lead to disciplinary measures, including termination. The computer use policy should also prohibit employees from sending or accessing pornography on the workplace computer. Once again, the policy should warn that violation of this portion of the policy would lead to disciplinary measures or termination.

It has been suggested by some legal commentators that employers should engage in a more aggressive approach to prevent the use of workplace computers in discrimination and creation of hostile work environment (Belanoff & Spelfogel, 1999). Some of these proposed measures include regular consensual monitoring of employee e-mail communication, purchase and installation of tracking or filtering software, and periodic random inspection of the printer area for obscene, derogatory, or pornographic materials. Although most of these measures would probably be legal, from a management standpoint many of these measures are ill-advised. It is an unremarkable proposition that good employee morale is one of the keys to productivity and loyalty to the employer. Employee morale is likely to hit an all-time low if the employer decides to engage in heavy-handed tactics in trying to prevent harassment or discrimination. Also, such actions may also become a drain on the employer's resources, particularly for small employers. Engaging in such aggressive tactics would require an employer to employ a full-time "cyber cop" or to have their human resources personnel devote a lot of time to these activities.

The best way to approach this issue is to have a policy that (a) encourages employees to bring any of their complaints or concerns to the attention of their supervisors, (b) requires employers to conduct a prompt and fair investigation of the allegations, (c) contemplates searches of the perpetrators' work computer in furtherance of that investigation, and (d) metes out appropriate discipline as necessary. Employers may also wish to conduct periodic training seminars on the etiquette of computer use in the work place. Such training could be made part of the orientation for all new employees.

E-mail communications and other computer files as evidence in litigation. In the last decade, e-mail communication has become a routine evidentiary item in court. For example, in a recent employment discrimination case, a California appellate court relied rather extensively on e-mail communication evidence to affirm a verdict in favor of the plaintiff (*Baratta v. Oracle Corp.,* 2002; see also *Costic v. Trammell Crow Co.,* 2003). Also, e-mail communication comments of LAPD Officer Lawrence Powell–"Oops, I haven't beaten anyone so bad in a long time"–were introduced in his criminal trial in the Rodney King case (Belanoff & Spelfogel, 1999).

Moreover, the courts have routinely granted litigants' request to access the opposing party's e-mail communications in discovery. For example, in a recent decision, a California appellate court ordered the plaintiff in a wrongful discharge case to produce to the defendant a home computer the plaintiff used to perform work for the defendant (*TBG Ins. Services. Corp. v. Superior Court,* 2002). Also, Rule 34 of the Federal Rules of Civil Procedure permits discovery of electronic records, such as e-mail communications. It should be noted that some courts have already taken the view that the expense of producing e-mail communication should be borne by the employer as a foreseeable cost of doing business. For example, in *In re Brand Name Prescription Drugs Antitrust Litigation* (1995), a federal court required the defendant drug manufacturer to produce over 30 million pages of e-mail communication at its own cost of $50,000 to $70,000.

However, an employer might find that *saving* certain e-mail communications or computer files from deletion helps it tremendously if its actions are later challenged in court.

The $64,000 question for the employer becomes which files and e-mail communications should be deleted and which should be saved. One of the most common myths among employers and employees is that when files and e-mail communications are deleted, they are wiped out of existence (Sidbury, 2001). But in reality, most of these files exist even after deletion on back up discs or tapes for the computer system until they are purged from the system permanently by the computer network administrator. That is why computer-savvy litigants now routinely include backup tapes into the list of documents requested in discovery. Also, as the number of backup tapes continues to grow, storage and space become issues.

Employers do have some options in dealing with the document retention dilemma. First, they should make all employees aware that any e-mail communications they send may become public and discoverable even if the employee intended his or her communication to be private. Therefore, employees should be asked not to put in an e-mail communication anything they would not put in a company memorandum. This warning is particularly true in businesses where confidentiality is paramount to protect the employer's trade or commercial secrets. Employers should also make all employees aware that any files or e-mail communications they delete do not actually disappear and might still be retrieved at a later time.

Employers should also develop and adopt a policy regarding e-mail communication retention and deletion. Pursuant to such a policy, employers should delete e-mail communication and purge them from any backup tapes on a periodic basis. In drafting such a policy, public employers should be aware that federal and state laws (such as, for example, the California Public Records Act) require the employer to preserve a copy of certain e-mail communications for the period specified in the law. It is probably a good idea for public employers to incorporate such laws into their e-mail communication retention and deletion policies by reference.

Finally, employers should instruct their employees that if they feel that a particular e-mail communication contains information vital to protect the employer's interests, that e-mail communication should be printed and put in the file. This approach would insure that truly important e-mail communications are preserved from periodic deletion.

CONCLUSION

Computers and the Internet are invaluable tools in the modern work place. The best way to ensure that these tools help employers become more successful and profitable is to carefully draft policies regarding proper computer and Internet use and electronic document retention and to require all employees to review the policies and evidence their understanding and acquiescence to these policies in writing. In drafting these policies, employers should remember that not every legally permissible employee monitoring tool amounts to a good business and management practice and that a healthy work environment is also a key to productivity and prosperity.

ACKNOWLEDGMENTS

The author of this article is a 1998 recipient of a Juris Doctorate Degree from Pepperdine University School of Law. The author is a former judicial staff attorney for the Honorable Art W. McKinster, California Court of Appeal, and a former judicial extern for the Honorable Stephen Reinhardt, U.S. Court of Appeals for the Ninth Circuit. The author is a practicing attorney admitted in the states of California and New York, and an associate at the law firm of LaMore, Brazier, Riddle &

Giampaoli in San Jose, California. The views expressed in this article do not represent LaMore, Brazier et al, or any of its clients.

REFERENCES

Baratta v. Oracle Corp. Cal.App. (2002) Unpub. LEXIS 4108.

Belanoff, E. J., & Spelfogel, E. J. (1999). E-mail communication: Property rights vs. privacy rights in the workplace. Retrieved March 31, 2004, from http://www.ebglaw.com/article_193.html

Bohach v. City of Reno, 932 F. Supp. 1232 (D. Nev. 1996).

Burton v. Wilmington Parking Authority 365 U.S. 715 (1961).

California v. Ciraolo 476 U.S. 207 (1986).

Clark v. Regents of University of California U.S. Dist. (1997) LEXIS 13182.

Costic v. Trammell Crow Co. Cal. App. (2003) Unpub. LEXIS 3363.

Electronic Communications Privacy Act of 1986, 18 U.S.C. A., § 2511.

In re Brand Name Prescription Drugs Antitrust Litigation, WL 360526 (N. D. Ill. 1995).

Katz v. United States, 389 U.S. 3471 (1967).

Li, H. H. (n.d.). Electronic mail privacy in the workplace. Retrieved March 31, 2004, from http://www.soc.neu.edu/archive/students/hanli.html

O'Connor v. Ortega, 480 U.S. 709 (1987).

Owens v. Morgan Stanley & Co., 96 Civ. 9747 (1997) Westlaw 403454 (S.D.N.Y. 12/24/1997).

Rosenbaum, J. (2001). In defense of the hard drive. *The Green Bag, 4*(2d), 169–172.

Sheffield v. Dept. of Soc. Serv. County of Los Angeles, 109 Cal.App.4th 153, 134 Cal.Rptr.2d 492 (2003).

Sidbury, B. F. (2001). You've got mail … and your boss knows it: Rethinking the scope of employer e-mail communication monitoring to the Electronic Communications Privacy Act, 2001 UCLA J. L. Tech. 5, p. 3.

TBG Ins. Services Corp. v. Superior Court, 96 Cal.App.4th 443, 117 Cal.Rptr.2d 155 (2002).

THE PSYCHOLOGIST-MANAGER JOURNAL, 2005, 8(2), 189–204

Employment Leasing Arrangements in the Context of Labor and Employment Laws

Lawrence J. Song and Jonathan M. Turner

Epstein, Turner & Song, P.C.

This article examines major federal labor and employment laws that impact on employment leasing arrangements. Employment leasing presents a complex maze of legal issues through which businesses must navigate. In cases where day-to-day control and supervision are reserved to the client firm, both the leasing firm and the client firm generally will be considered to be the "joint employer" of the leased employees. The legal significance of this term is explained in this article in the context of specific federal labor and employment laws, revealing the hidden hazards of employment leasing arrangements.

Like employees, employers come in all shapes and sizes; a business model that works for one employer may not work for another. Although one may quarrel over what is an appropriate business model for a particular employer, all would agree that a primary objective of any business model is efficiency and that, as a general rule, reducing operating costs can be a step towards achieving that objective.

Recently, more employers have begun to examine "outsourcing" in an attempt to effect cost reductions. Generally speaking, outsourcing involves the contracting-out of those portions of an employer's operation which the employer has neither the time nor the expertise to manage comfortably or efficiently. As the growth of service industries continues to outpace that of the manufacturing industries, product outsourcing is being overshadowed by employment outsourcing. A relatively new concept in employment outsourcing services is "employment leasing." Although employment leasing programs can vary from one leasing firm to the next, their primary selling point for the prospective client is this: for a negotiated

Correspondence should be sent to Lawrence J. Song, Epstein, Turner & Song, P. C., 5750 Wilshire Blvd., Suite 560, Los Angeles, CA 90036. E-mail: ljs@etslaw.com

fee, the leasing firm agrees to be the "employer of record" for persons working at the client's facilities. In this capacity, the leasing firm will handle all of the bureaucratic paperwork associated with the hiring of employees, the tracking of pay hours and benefits accrual, payroll taxes, worker's compensation insurance, unemployment insurance, job safety programs, I–9 requirements, and other labor and employment law requirements. Depending on the needs of the client and the industry involved, the leasing firm also might maintain day-to-day control and supervision over the leased employees. In cases where day-to-day control and supervision are reserved to the client firm, both the leasing firm and the client firm generally will be considered to be the "joint employer" of the leased employees. The legal significance of this term will be explained further below as we discuss the various workplace laws that are the subject of this article.

Although employment leasing can be an attractive possibility for many businesses, it also can present a complex maze of legal issues through which businesses must navigate. In this article, we will examine some of the major labor and employment laws of which both the leasing firm and the client firm should be aware, and how such laws can impact on the respective rights and obligations of the parties on either side of this business arrangement.

WORKER ADJUSTMENT AND RETRAINING NOTIFICATION ACT

In the wake of numerous plant closings and mergers in the 1970's and 1980's, Congress passed the *Worker's Adjustment Retraining And Notification Act* in 1988 (the WARN Act). The WARN Act affords certain advance notice protections to workers in the event that an employer orders a plant closing or mass layoff. Under the Act, companies who know that they will be closing their doors and laying off employees generally must give 60 days notice of this event to their employees, to allow employees and their families "some transition time to adjust to the prospective loss of employment, to seek and obtain alternative jobs, and, if necessary, to enter skilled training or retraining that will allow these workers to successfully compete in the job market" (WARN Act, 20 C.F.R.§639.1[a]).

In the case of employment leasing arrangements, the question of whether the leasing firm, the client firm, or both are considered an employer for WARN purposes has significance for a number of reasons. First, whether an employer is subject to WARN Act obligations will depend on the size of its workforce and the number of employees affected by the plant closing or mass layoff. The WARN Act covers employers with 100 or more employees and the threshold number for a mass layoff under the Act ranges from a minimum of 50 employees to a maximum of 500, depending on the size of the overall workforce. In the employment leasing arrangement, there can be circumstances where, if either of the two business entities had been considered alone, a WARN Act violation might not be found, either because that entity by itself did not employ the required number of employees to trigger WARN coverage or because the number of employees terminated as a result of a plant closing or mass layoff did not meet the required threshold to trigger the notice obligation.

Even if it could be established that one of the entities by itself has the required number of employees to trigger employer coverage or to meet the mass layoff definition under the WARN Act, it still may be imprudent from the point of view of plaintiffs' counsel to pursue relief only against that one entity. Remember, the very events that trigger WARN Act obligations are events that typify, or are characteristic of, a business operating under precarious financial conditions. Hence, plaintiffs' counsel will likely look for additional, "deeper pocket" defendants from which to recover, including any defendants who can arguably be said to be a joint employer of the affected employees.

The following hypothetical case illustrates how the previous issues can come into play. Suppose an employment leasing firm has a nationwide business servicing both large and small clients. One of its clients is a recent startup operation that has need for additional personnel to augment its current workforce of 35 employees. The leasing firm places 20 persons at the client's facility. These 20 persons report their hours and submit time records to the leasing firm; however, their work is directly supervised on site by managers employed by the client firm. If there are performance or disciplinary problems with the leased employee, the managers must contact the leasing firm, who then addresses the problem directly with the employee.

Some time after the leased employees begin working at the client's facility, the client, short on cash resources, determines that it no longer can afford to keep the facility open. If the client should close the facility and layoff all of the workers, are the affected employees entitled to the 60-day notice under the WARN Act? On the one hand, it can be argued that the client firm, who only has 35 employees on its own payroll, does not meet the threshold number of employees (50) to qualify as a covered employer under the Act; yet, on the other hand, there is no question that if the facility is closed, the total number of employees affected (55) meets the threshold number required under the Act's definition of a plant closure.

The WARN Act does not directly address the issues presented by this hypothetical; however, the Department of Labor has issued regulations intended as a guide for determining when two or more business entities might be taken into consideration for purposes of determining employer obligations under the WARN Act (20 C.F.R.§639.3[a][2]; 54 Fed. Reg. 16042, 16045, 1989). These regulations, which are broad enough to cover employment leasing arrangements, essentially adopt a five-factor analysis to be considered along with other factors borrowed from existing state corporation law and various federal labor laws, notably the *National Labor Relations Act* (NLRA, 29 U.S.C.§ 151 et seq., 1935). Thus, the regulations consider whether and to what extent the two entities have common ownership, directors, or officers; defacto exercise of control; unity of personnel policies emanating from a common source; and a dependency of operations.

Under the NLRA, federal courts as well as the National Labor Relations Board have held that day-to-day control over business operations and labor relations are the most important factors for determining whether two or more entities are considered to be a single employer, or at least joint employers. Consequently, there are many NLRA cases which have found that when, as in the above hypothetical, an employment leasing firm refers out employees to a client that provides on-site supervision over these employees, both may be considered to be a joint employer of the employees. Even so, a joint employer finding in this case does not end the analysis for WARN Act purposes. If the client firm had made the decision to close its facility without consulting with or giving advance notice to the leasing firm, it is likely that the leasing firm will not be liable under the WARN Act for failing to provide employees with the advance notice thereunder (*Administaff Companies, Inc. v. New York*, 2003). In this case, the statute imposes liability only on an employer who orders the closing of a plant.

Obviously, such a result might not sit well with the client firm because, in many employment leasing arrangements, the leasing firm will market itself as being knowledgeable about employer compliance obligations with respect to the various federal and state labor and employment laws. In the previous hypothetical, one can easily anticipate the arguments that would be made by the client firm in the event that that firm was sued under the WARN Act: the very reason that the client firm, a small startup operation, retained the leasing firm was because the client firm was not knowledgeable about human resource management and compliance obligations and therefore was looking to the leasing firm's professed expertise for guidance and direction on this subject.

To avoid litigation of these and related issues it is, of course, important that in any employment leasing arrangement the leasing firm and the client clarify in advance the respective obligations and responsibilities that each agrees to assume in the arrangement. Appropriate indemnification and "hold harmless" provisions should be negotiated and set forth in a signed writing between the parties. Experienced labor and employment counsel should be consulted prior to finalizing the arrangement.

FAMILY AND MEDICAL LEAVE ACT

In 1993 Congress passed the *Family and Medical Leave Act* (FMLA), which mandates that employers provide up to 12 weeks of unpaid leave to employees who request time off because of certain qualifying events under the Act. The qualifying events include childbirth (and post-delivery care), adoption, the care of a family member who has a serious health condition, or the employee's own serious health condition. While on FMLA leave, employees are entitled to continued health coverage (if the employer provided such coverage for its other employees). Further, upon their return from FMLA leave, employees must be restored to their former position or an equivalent position "with equivalent benefits, pay and other terms and conditions of employment" (29 U.S.C. §2614[a][1]).

As with other federal labor and employment laws, FMLA leave issues can arise in connection with the question of who is the employer under business arrangements between employment leasing firms and client firms. This is because the FMLA coverage applies to employers with 50 or more employees within a 75-mile radius of a specific employer location and because employees are not eligible for FMLA leave unless they have been employed for at least 1,250 hr within a 12-month period by the employer from whom leave is requested. Here again, there can be situations in an employment leasing arrangement where, if only one or the other business entity were examined alone, FMLA obligations would not be triggered, either because the business entity did not employ the requisite number of employees within a 75-mile radius or because the particular employee seeking FMLA leave did not have the required hours and length of service with the employer "with respect to whom leave is requested" (29 U.S.C. §2611[2][A][i]).

To appreciate how such issues can arise, we will use another case illustration, this time based on actual events taken from a recent federal case. In *Phillips v. LeRoy, Somer North American* (2003), the employee began working at a manufacturing plant through a temporary agency, with the understanding that the employee would transition to a regular employee of the manufacturing company after a period of satisfactory job performance.

After a trial period, she became the exclusive employee of the manufacturing firm. Subsequently, she became unable to do her job due to complications from a pregnancy. She requested medical leave and was approved for short-term disability. After her child was born, her doctor did not release her to return to work for several weeks. She received short-term disability benefits for almost 22 consecutive weeks. It was the employer's policy that, if an employee were eligible for both short-term disability and FMLA leave, both types of leave would run concurrently.

Upon the employee's return to work, she was told that her position was no longer available and she was given a choice of several alternative jobs. She chose the only job available on the first shift, which was the shift she had worked on prior to her leave. This job paid less than the job she held before commencing leave. Eventually, the employee was laid off.

The employee sued the manufacturing firm under the FMLA, alleging that this employer violated the FMLA by failing to reinstate her to her previous position or to an equivalent position. The manufacturing firm defended upon the ground that the employee did not meet the FMLA's eligibility requirement, which required that employees be employed "for at least 12 months by the employer with respect to whom leave is requested" (29 U.S.C. § 2611[2][A][i]). In making the argument against eligibility, the manufacturing firm excluded the time that the employee had worked at the plant as an employee of the temporary agency. The court held that this time could not be excluded. In reaching this conclusion, the court relied on 29 C.F.R.§825.106 which the Secretary of Labor issued to address joint-employer arrangements. The regulations provide that "where two or more businesses exercise some control over the work or working conditions of the employee," these employees could be considered to be "jointly employed" by both businesses and, as such, "must be counted by both employers, whether or not maintained on one employer's payroll, in determining employer coverage and employee eligibility [under the FMLA]."

The FMLA regulations further state that "a joint employment relationship ... is determined [not] by the application of any single criteria, but rather the entire relationship is to be viewed in its totality" (29 C.F.R. § 825.106[b]). The regulation gives as an example of a joint employment situation where "a temporary or leasing agency supplies employees to a second employer." Because federal courts typically defer to regulations issued by a federal agency charged with the responsibility to interpret and enforce a particular law, it was not surprising that the court in the *Phillips* case found that the employee was entitled to rely on her combined service with the employment leasing firm and the client firm to determine eligibility for FMLA leave (*Miller v. Defiance Metal Productions, Inc.* 1997; *Solgado v. CDW Computer Centers, Inc.,* 1975, 1998).

This is not to say that there is a blanket rule mandating that the client firm must always extend FMLA coverage to persons providing their services through a leasing arrangement. As the regulations state, each arrangement must be examined on a case-by-case basis, taking into consideration the "totality of the evidence" (*Moreau v. Air France,* 2004, 942). Hence, if the employment leasing arrangement is constructed in such a way that the leasing firm retains the day-to-day control and supervision over the workers, determines their rates of pay, sets their work schedules, and keeps their employment records, then the fact that the client firm will occasionally give instruction to these workers may not be sufficient to establish an FMLA obligation as between the client firm and the worker. Still, the on-site client should avoid, as much as possible, giving work assignments and instructions directly to the worker; those instructions instead should be communicated to the employment leasing firm's representative. In turn, the employment leasing firm ideally should have a representative on site or readily available to receive such communications from the client, so that at all times the day-to-day supervision is being effected by the leasing firm. It is not uncommon for leasing firms to maintain permanent offices on site at the client firm's premises precisely for this purpose.

Experienced labor and employment counsel should be consulted when formalizing these arrangements.

FAIR LABOR STANDARDS ACT

In 1938 Congress passed the *Fair Labor Standards Act* (FLSA) to correct and eliminate those "conditions detrimental to the maintenance of the minimum standard of living necessary for health, efficiency, and general well-being of workers 29 U.S.C. § 2101, et seq." The FLSA established a minimum wage, regulations concerning maximum hours, record-keeping and reporting requirements, child labor provisions, and a system of civil and criminal penalties for FLSA violations (*Torres-Lopez v. May,* 1997).

Aside from the minimum wage, which is set by the Department of Labor, the primary rights and obligations under the FLSA arise from its regulation of maximum work hours and overtime compensation. Under the FLSA, no employer may employ any employee for a workweek longer than 40 hr unless the employee receives overtime compensation at a rate of 1 ½ times his or her regular rate of pay. Some states also have their own daily overtime rules in addition to weekly overtime rules. The FLSA does not regulate daily overtime.

Like the WARN Act and the FMLA, the FLSA's statutory text does not purport to describe every conceivable business arrangement that could qualify as an employment relationship under which FLSA rights and obligations attach, nor does the statutory text speak directly to employment leasing arrangements. However, the courts historically have observed that the "remedial purposes" of the FLSA require courts to define employment relationships in the broadest possible manner (*Baystate Alternative Staffing, Inc. v. Herman,* 1998; *Preston v. Settle Down Enterprises, Inc.,* 2000; *Rutherford Food Corp. v. McComb,* 1947; *Torres-Lopez v. May,* 1997). Towards that end, there is no question today that "[t]he FLSA contemplates several simultaneous employers each responsible for compliance with the Act" (*Baystate Alternative Staffing, Inc. v. Herman,* 1998, 668).

In the typical employment leasing arrangement, both the leasing firm and the client firm have characteristics of employer status; thus, although the employment leasing firm typically maintains employee time records and other personnel records and pays the employees' compensation and benefits, as a practical matter the client firm almost always exercises the day-to-day control and on-site supervision over the employees. Under these circumstances, the courts will not hesitate to find that both entities are deemed to be the employer for purposes of compliance with the minimum wage and overtime requirements under the FLSA (*Baystate,* 1998; *Preston,* 2000). Department of Labor regulations and policy statements also confirm this view ("Employment Relationship Under the Fair Labor Standards Act," 2005).

Another case illustration, again based on facts taken from a recent federal case, helps demonstrate how these issues can arise under the FLSA (*Baystate,* 1998). In that case, the defendants formed and operated a number of "temp agencies" (employment leasing firms) to service clients in need of unskilled labor to perform industrial and factory work, heavy labor, and assembly and packing. The leasing firms generally charged the client firms between $6.00 and $7.50 per hr for the services of the workers; from this amount, the leasing firms usually paid the workers the minimum wage, keeping the premium for themselves. In an apparent effort to avoid having to pay overtime wages to the workers, the leasing firms had each worker sign a "contractor agreement," which purported to designate each worker as an "independent contractor" and not an employee.

Following an audit by the Department of Labor, the leasing firms were assessed civil penalties in the amount of $150,000 for willful violations of the FLSA's overtime provisions. The leasing firms sought review of this decision in federal court. Although eventually conceding that the workers were not really independent contractors, the leasing firms argued that the workers were only the employees of the client firms for whom they performed labor, rather than the leasing firms' employees. The court was unpersuaded by this argument for a number of reasons. The court noted that the leasing firms were solely responsible for hiring the workers, they had the power to refuse to send a worker back to a job site where he or she performed unsatisfactorily, they supervised and controlled the employee work schedules and conditions of employment, they dictated the times at which workers were to report to the temp agency offices, they screened workers for minimum qualifications, they decided which workers would be assigned to particular job sites, they sometimes transported workers to job sites at client companies, they instructed workers about appropriate dress and work habits, and they forbade workers from contacting directly a client company about potential job opportunities.

From these facts, it was no surprise that the court had little trouble concluding that the workers were employees of the leasing firms; however, the more remarkable observation is that, even with all of the employer characteristics attributed to the leasing firms, the court still indicated that the client firms also had "simultaneous employer status" (*Baystate*, 1998, 676). Hence, the client firms arguably could have been jointly and severally liable for the overtime violations, despite the fact that the leasing firms had set the work schedules, and presumably maintained the timesheets and pay records for the workers. In this case, liability of the client firms no doubt would have been based on the fact that the client firms exercised direct, on-the-job supervision over the workers.

The above case once again demonstrates why employment leasing firms and client firms should clarify their respective rights and obligations to each other in advance, and memorialize those rights and obligations in writing before finalizing their business arrangement. In fact, this is a subject of particular importance where the FLSA is concerned. Given the broad remedial purposes that gave rise to the passage of the FLSA, courts are more inclined to find the existence of an employment relationship for FLSA purposes even though such a relationship might not exist for purposes of other federal labor laws. For example, in determining the existence of an employment relationship under the FLSA, the courts apply an "economic realities" test that takes into consideration the remedial nature of the legislation and whether the person pursuing an FLSA claim is "economically dependent" on his or her alleged employer (*Baystate*, 1998; *Torres-Lopez*, 1997). In contrast, for purposes of Title VII of the *Civil Rights Act of 1964* and the NLRA, the courts have rejected this test and have instead applied a common law test when determining whether an employment relationship exists. For example, in determining the existence of an employment relationship under the FLSA, the courts apply an economic realities test that takes into consideration the remedial nature of the legislation, and whether the person pursuing an FLSA claim is economically dependent on his or her alleged employer (*Baystate*, 1998; *Torres-Lopez*, 1997). When determining whether an employment relationship exists for purposes of Title VII (the primary federal law prohibiting employment discrimination) and the NLRA (the primary federal law protecting and regulating union organizing rights), the courts have rejected this test and have instead applied a common law test.

NATIONAL LABOR RELATIONS ACT

In 1935, Congress passed the *National Labor Relations Act* (NLRA), which gives employees the right to form, join, or assist labor unions; to bargain collectively with their employer through a union or other representative they have selected; or to engage in other similar concerted activity. Under the NLRA, it is an unfair labor practice for an employer to interfere with, restrain or coerce employees in the exercise of these rights. It also is an unfair labor practice for an employer to discriminate against employees because of their union sympathies or support. In addition to conducting elections to determine whether employees wish to be unionized, the NLRB investigates and prosecutes unfair labor practice charges.

Although the NLRA does not directly speak to employment leasing arrangements, the NLRB and the courts have developed a body of law to address such arrangements under the joint-employer doctrine. Under that doctrine, two distinct, separately owned enterprises are considered joint employers if they share or codetermine matters governing essential terms and conditions of employment (*NLRB v. Browning-Ferris Industries, Inc.*, 1982; *Riverdale Nursing Home*, 1995). The doctrine has been applied both in NLRB election cases and unfair labor practice cases.

Can the client firm terminate the leasing arrangement to avoid the union? If the client firm and the leasing firm are found to be joint employers under NLRB standards, the answer is "no" (*Whitewood Maintenance Co.*, 1989). As already noted, the NLRA prohibits employer discrimination against employees because of their union activities. Generally, when an employer makes a business decision that results in the termination of its employees, it will be held to answer to the NLRB for having committed an unfair labor practice if the reason for the decision was based on anti-union sentiment (*Textile Workers v. Darlington Manufacturing Co.*, 1965).

This case resulted in a holding that an employer "has an absolute right to terminate his entire business for any reason he pleases" (Darlington Manufacturing Co., p. 268), even if done with antiunion animus. This is true even if the affected employees also may have been jointly employed by someone else and could be reassigned elsewhere by the other employer. But what about the leasing firm? Would the leasing firm who suffered economically and against its will due to the termination of the lease be liable as well? One case held that only the client firm is liable for the unfair labor practice (*Computer Associates International, Inc.*, 2000). Even so, the answer still may be "yes," if the leasing firm failed to take all measures within its power to resist the unlawful action.

If the leasing firm and client firm are not considered joint employers under NLRB standards, can the client firm terminate the leasing arrangement for antiunion reasons? Remarkably, the NLRB has ruled "yes," under the theory that any business may cease doing business with another business, even if the reason is because of the union activities of the latter's employees. Even here, however, the NLRB has consistently held that a client firm cannot direct, instruct, or order the leasing firm to terminate specific employees of the leasing firm for antiunion reasons (*Dews Construction Corp.*, 1977; *Esmark, Inc.*, 1994; *Georgia-Pacific Corp.*, 1975).

The foregoing scenarios are illustrative of a common and frequently litigated question in employment leasing cases under the NLRA: whether the leasing firm, the client firm, or both are responsible for remedying an unfair labor practice committed by only one of the entities. Under NLRB policy, if both entities are found to be joint employers of the affected employees, then even the nonacting entity could be held responsible for remedying the unfair labor practice if (a) that entity knew or should have known that the other acted for unlawful reasons and (b) the non-acting entity acquiesced in the unlawful conduct by failing to protest it or to exercise any contractual right it might have to resist it (*Capital EMI Music, Inc.*, 1993).

In the end, whether or not a joint-employer relationship exists between the leasing firm and the client firm, both entities must proceed with extreme caution whenever it appears that business or personnel decisions are being considered in response to union activity. If it ultimately turns out that one or both entities acted unlawfully, significant exposure could materialize. The NLRB remedial powers are broad. Depending on the circumstances, the NLRB could order both entities to make employees whole for back pay and lost benefits caused by unfair labor practices attributed to both. If a lease termination was involved, the NLRB could order reinstatement of the lease. Both entities also could be ordered to "cease and desist" in the commission of any further unfair labor practices. NLRB orders generally are enforceable following a review process with the federal courts of appeal. An employer who fails to comply with an NLRB order following such review is subject to federal court contempt proceedings (*NLRB v. Deena Artware, Inc.*, 1960).

EQUAL EMPLOYMENT OPPORTUNITY LAWS

Title VII of *The Civil Rights Act of 1964* marked the beginning of a series of federal laws aimed at providing equal employment opportunity in the workplace. Uniformly, the equal employment opportunity laws prohibit employers from discriminating against job applicants and employees in connection with hiring, compensation, and other terms and conditions of employment. In addition to Title VII, the major federal statutes in this category include the *Age Discrimination in Employment Act* (ADEA, 1967) and the *Americans with Disabilities Act* (ADA, 1990). The Equal Employment Opportunity Commission (EEOC) is the federal agency primarily responsible for the administrative enforcement of Title VII, ADEA, and ADA.

Title VII prohibits workplace discrimination based on race, color, religion, sex (which includes discrimination because of pregnancy, childbirth, or related medical conditions), or national origin. The ADEA prohibits workplace discrimination against persons aged 40 or over. The ADA prohibits workplace discrimination against any "otherwise qualified" person who has a physical or mental disability, that is, any person who, with or without reasonable accommodation of the disability, can perform the essential functions of the job in question. Although workplace harassment is not specifically mentioned in any of these laws, the courts by and large have held that harassment of employees in any of the groups protected by these laws constitutes unlawful discrimination (*Huang v. Gruner Jahr USA Publishing*, 2000; *McCowan v. All Star Maintenance, Inc.*, 2001; *Neudecker v. Boisclair Corp.*, 2003; *Rivera-Rodriguez v. Frito Lay Snacks Caribbean*, 2001; *Shanoff v. Illinois Dept. of Human Services,* 2001).

Harassment has been broadly defined as severe or pervasive conduct or actions that reasonably would be viewed as offensive from the perspective of the members of a protected group (*Meritor Savings Bank, FSB v. Vinson*, 1986).

As with the other laws discussed ealier, the equal employment opportunity laws utilize joint-employer principles to determine liability of the respective parties to an employment leasing arrangement. Here again, although courts differ in the precise test to be applied to determine joint-employer status, the essential factual inquiry is whether one or both entities control the day-to-day activities of the employees in question (*Armbruster v. Quinn*, 1983). Other courts apply a combination of the common law right-to-control factors with the economic realities of the working relationship of the employee (*Cobb v. Sun Papers, Inc.*, 1982; *EEOC v. Zippo Mfg. Co.*,1983; *Garrett v. Phillips Mills, Inc.*,1983; *Lutcher v. Musicians Union Local 47*, 1980; *Mares v. Marsh*,1985; *Oestman v. National Farmers Union Ins. Co.*, 1992; *Unger v. Consolidated Foods Corp.*,1981; cert. denied, 1983).

The EEOC has issued enforcement guidelines to address the rapidly growing phenomenon of employment leasing arrangements (EEOC, 1997). The guidelines enumerate several factors that should be taken into consideration to determine when there is a sufficient degree of day-to-day control shared by the leasing firm and the client firm vis à vis the leased employees such that a joint-employment relationship exists.

When a joint-employer relationship is found to exist under the equal employment opportunity laws, additional questions may arise as to which workers are counted for purposes of determining whether there is even coverage under the respective laws. Title VII applies to employers who employ 15 or more employees, the ADEA applies to employers who employ 20 or more employees, and the ADA applies to employers who employ 15 or more employees. The general rule is that the leasing firm and the client firm must each count all employees with whom they have an employment relationship (*Walters v. Metropolitan Education Enterprises, Inc.*, 1997).

Assuming there is statutory coverage over both of the joint employers, the EEOC guidelines provide that both are liable for the combined discriminatory practices, and are individually and jointly liable for back pay, front pay, and compensatory damages. The EEOC guidance (1997) also provides that punitive damages can be assessed against each employer in accordance with their respective degree of malicious or reckless conduct.

As with the other laws discussed earlier, the equal employment opportunity laws can present unique and complex issues when applied to employment leasing arrangements. Consider, for example, the following scenario. Leasco is a leasing firm that employs workers who have been assigned to a client firm. Although the client firm exercises no control over the workers' terms and conditions of employment, it has the right under its leasing arrangement to ask for a replacement worker if the client firm is not happy with the services of a worker presently assigned to the client. As with any service business, the success of Leasco's business depends on its ability to keep its clients satisfied; consequently, when the client firm makes a request for a replacement worker, Leasco makes every effort to accommodate the request. But what happens when the replaced worker sues, believing that the client firm's request and her removal was motivated by her race? A prudent plaintiff's attorney probably will sue both entities under Title VII but can the suit succeed against the client firm if that entity was not the plaintiff's employer? After all, the general rule is that an employment relationship must exist between the defendant and the plaintiff before that plaintiff can recover under Title VII (*Anderson v. Pacific Maritime Association*, 2003; *EEOC v. Pacific Maritime Association*, 2003).

Can the suit succeed against Leasco if Leasco had no racial bias against the plaintiff but merely sought to accommodate the client firm's request?

According to the EEOC's enforcement guidelines, the client firm can be liable in the previous scenario, even though it is not the plaintiff's employer (*Miland v. Bil-Mar Foods*, 1998; *Sibley Mem. Hosp. V. Wilson*, 1973). This is because Title VII prohibits not just discrimination by an employer but also interference with any individual in the exercise or enjoyment of any right granted or protected under the

Act (*Miland v. Bil-Mar Foods*, 1998; *Sibley Mem. Hosp. V. Wilson*, 1973). Nor is Leasco off the hook if facts suggest that it knew or suspected that the reason for the client's request for a replacement worker was racially motivated. "Client preference" or "client sensitivity" is not a defense to hiring or firing decisions or other personnel actions under the equal employment opportunity laws, even if the employer itself did not harbor any unlawful bias or prejudice against the plaintiff (*EEOC v. Recruit*, 1991).

Client sensitivity also is not a defense to a harassment case under these laws. Consider the following scenario based in part on an actual case. A leasing firm assigned one of its employees to a client firm's office to work as the building manager for one of the client firm's apartment buildings. During a meeting at the client firm's offices, the president of the client firm made unwanted and sexually explicit comments to the building manager in the presence of the leasing firm's managing director, who did nothing to address the incident. After unsuccessful attempts to get the leasing firm to admonish the client firm's president, the building manager sued both the leasing firm and the client firm for sexual harassment.

Should the leasing firm be held responsible for the acts of the client firm's president, even though these were acts taken by a person not employed by the leasing firm, and even though these acts occurred away from the leasing firm's work site? According to one court, the answer is yes. The court concluded that the leasing firm could be liable if it knew or should have known about the offending conduct but failed to take prompt and immediate action. The court stated that the leasing firm could have deterred the president of the client firm and his alleged sexual harassment; unfortunately, how such deterrence could have been accomplished was a matter that the court left to the parties' imagination (*Kudatzky v. Galbreath Co.*, 1997). Although the leasing firm clearly should have investigated the building manager's complaint, as a practical matter, the leasing firm had no power or authority to discipline the president of the client firm. Nor would it have been practical or realistic for the leasing firm to bring the harassment issue up at the client firm's next board meeting.

Other options that were available to the leasing firm would have presented similar challenges. For example, how effective would it be if the leasing firm confronted the president of the client firm and demanded that he immediately stop his unlawful conduct? How effective or practical would it be for the leasing firm to threaten the client firm that it would terminate its services if there were one more incident of inappropriate behavior toward the building manager? How likely would it be that the client firm terminate the leasing arrangement? What would the consequences be if the victim found herself without a job because she complained about unlawful harassment? Would reassignment of the building manager to another client firm solve the problem? Perhaps not, if the victim viewed the reassignment as punitive or less desirable. Would assigning a male worker to the client firm solve the problem? There are obvious sex discrimination issues presented by this option.

The EEOC and the courts have developed certain legal principles by which all employers can be guided when faced with the dilemma of how to address inappropriate comments or behavior occurring in workplace settings in which the employer does not have complete control. It is important to bear in mind that the equal employment opportunity laws do not impose a legal obligation on employers to guarantee a work place free of unlawful harassment; what is required is that the employer take all reasonable measures to prevent harassment from occurring and to promptly correct for it when it does occur (*Shaw v. AutoZone, Inc.*, 1999).

Under this standard, although the leasing firm in the previous case was, without question, obligated to take some kind of action to address the harassment of the building manager, the courts probably would be sympathetic to a solution that seeks to avoid unwarranted confrontation or disruption of business relations with the client, as long as the solution decided on does not compromise the victim's rights. Here, if the leasing firm is not prepared to terminate business relations with the client firm, the practical solution perhaps would be to reassign the worker to a comparable client firm, with no loss in pay or benefits, reiterate the leasing firm's commitment to having a work environment free of harassment, and assure the building manager that there will be no retaliation for her complaint of harassment. However, the leasing firm also must bear in mind the fact that it now has knowledge that this particular client has engaged in inappropriate conduct against one of the leasing firm's employees, and that any future acts of a similar nature could present major legal consequences. This risk should be carefully assessed with counsel.

CONCLUSION

We have not attempted to present an exhaustive review of workplace laws relevant to employment leasing. In addition to the laws discussed, employment leasing arrangements can be the subject of joint-employer liability issues arising under the *Occupational Safety and Health Act* (29 U.S.C. § 651 et seq., 1970), which regulates matters concerning workplace safety. The Occupational Safety and Health Review Commission has stated that even where a borrowing company has agreed to accept responsibility, "an employer remains accountable for the health and safety of its employees, wherever they work, and cannot divest itself of its obligations under the [Occupational Safety and Health Act] by contracting its responsibility to another employer" (*Secretary v. Acchione & Canuso, Inc.*, 1980).

Also relevant are the *Employee Retirement Income Security Act* (29 U.S.C. § 1001, et seq., 1974), which regulates the administration of retirement, health or other fringe benefit plans established or maintained by an employer (*Central States, Southeast and Southwest Areas Pensions Fund v. Central Transport*, 1996), and the federal tax laws (*General Motors Corp. v. United States*, 1990). Internal

Revenue Code §3401(d; 2005) essentially allows the parties to an employment leasing arrangement to allocate federal employment tax responsibilities to the leasing firm, even if the firm fails to qualify as a common law employer, so long as the firm maintains control of the payment of wages to workers.

There are state labor and employment laws that impact on employment leasing arrangements. Though we have not traversed the entire legal landscape affecting the business relations between employment leasing firms and client firms, we hope that this article provides insight into the juxtaposition of the federal laws discussed and employment leasing arrangements.

ACKNOWLEDGMENTS

Lawrence J. Song and Jonathan M. Turner are partners at the law firm Epstein, Turner & Song in Los Angeles, California. Mr. Song specializes in employment law and labor relations for management. Mr. Turner specializes in employment law, labor relations law, and business litigation.

The contents and the views set forth in this article represent the authors' 50 years of collective experience in the practice of labor and employment law. It is in no way intended to constitute or provide legal advice, or to substitute for legal counsel. This article does not address workplace laws of specific states, which may significantly differ from the federal laws discussed herein.

REFERENCES

Administaff Companies, Inc. v. New York Jt. Bd., Shirt & Leisure Div; 337 F.3d 454, 457 (5th Cir. 2003).
Age Discrimination in Employment Act, 29 U.S.C. § 631 (1967).
Americans with Disabilities Act, 42 U.S.C. § 12111(5)(A) (1990).
Anderson v. Pacific Maritime Association 336 F.3d 924 (9th Cir.2003).
Armbruster v. Quinn, 711 F.2d 1332, 1340, 1341 & n. 7 (6th Cir.1983).
Baystate Alternative Staffing, Inc., supra citing Falk v. Brennan (1973) 414 US 190, 195, 94 S.Ct. 427.
Baystate Alternative Staffing v. Herman, 163 F.3d 668, 675, 676 (1st Cir.1998).
Capital EMI Music, Inc., 311 NLRB 997 (1993).
Central States, Southeast and Southwest Areas Pensions Fund v. Central Transport, Incorporated, 85 F.3d 1282 (7th Cir. 1996).
The Civil Rights Act of 1964, 42 U.S.C. § 2000e.
Cobb v. Sun Papers, Inc., 673 F.2d 337, 340–41 (11th Cir.), cert. denied (1982).
Computer Associates International, Inc., 332 NLRB No. 108 (2000), enf. denied, 282 F.3d 849.
Dews Construction Corp., 231 NLRB 182 (1977).
Employee Retirement Income Security Act, 29 U.S.C. § 1001, et seq., 1974.
Equal Employment Opportunity Commission. (1997, Dec. 3). Enforcement Guidance: Application of EEO Laws to Contingent Workers Placed by Temporary Employment Agencies and other Staffing Firms, 1997 WL 33159161.

Equal Employment Opportunity Commission v. Pacific Maritime Association (9th Cir.2003) 351 F.3d 1270.

Equal Employment Opportunity Commission v. Recruit U.S.A., Inc., 939 F.2d 746 (9th Cir. 1991).

Equal Employment Opportunity Commission v. Zippo Mfg. Co., 713 F.2d 32, 37–38 (3d Cir.1983).

Employment relationship under the Fair Labor Standards Act (FLSA). Retrieved on 3/9/05 from http:// www.dol.gov/esa/regs/compliance/whd/whdfs13.htm

Esmark, Inc., 315 NLRB 763 (1994).

Fair Labor Standards Act, 29 U.S.C. § 204(f) (1938), 29 C. F. R. § 791.2(a) (1938).

Family and Medical Leave Act, 29 U.S.C. § 2601 et seq., 2611, 2614 (1993), 29 C.F.R. §825.106 (1993).

Garrett v. Phillips Mills, Inc., 721 F.2d 979, 981–82 (4th Cir.1983).

General Motors Corp. v. United States, 1990 WL 259676 (E.D. Mich. 1990) 496 US 530 (1990).

Georgia-Pacific Corp., 221 NLRB 982 (1975).

Huang v. Gruner Jahr USA Publishing, 2000 W.L. 1371343 (S.D.N.Y. 2000).

Internal Revenue Code 3401(d), 26 U. S. C. 3401(d) (2005).

Kudatzky v. Galbreath Co., W.L. 598586 (S.D.N.Y. 1997).

Lutcher v. Musicians Union Local 47, 633 F.2d 880, 883 & n. 5 (9th Cir.1980).

Mares v. Marsh, 777 F.2d 1066, 1067–68 & n. 2 (5th Cir.1985).

McCowan v. All Star Maintenance, Inc., 273 F.3d 917 (10th Cir. 2001).

Meritor Savings Bank, FSB v. Vinson, 477 U.S. 57–62–66 (1986).

Miland v. Bil-Mar Foods, 994 F. Supp 1061 (N.D. Iowa 1998).

Miller v. Defiance Metal Productions, Inc. (ND Ohio 1997) 989 F.Supp.945, 947–48.

Moreau v. Air France, 356 F.3d 942 (9th Cir. 2004).

National Labor Relations Act of 1935, 29 U.S.C. § 141 (1935).

National Labor Relations Board v. Browning-Ferris Industries, Inc., 691 F.2d 1117 (3d Cir. 1982).

National Labor Relations Board v. Deena Artware, Inc., 361 U.S. 398, 80 S.Ct. 441 (1960).

Neudecker v. Boisclair Corp., 351 F.3d 361 (8th Cir. 2003).

Occupation Safety and Health Act, 29 U.S.C. § 651 et seq., 1970.

Oestman v. National Farmers Union Ins. Co., 958 F.2d 303, 305 (10th Cir.1992).

Phillips v. LeRoy, Somer North American (WD Tenn. 2003) 2003 WL 1790941 (unpublished opinion).

Preston v. Settle Down Enterprises, Inc. (ND GA 2000) 90 F.Supp2d 1267, 1273–1274.

Rivera-Rodriguez v. Frito Lay Snacks Caribbean, 265 F. 3d 15 (1st Cir. 2001).

Riverdale Nursing Home, 317 NLRB 881 (1995).

Rutherford Food Corp. v. McComb (1947) 331US 722, 67 S.Ct. 1473.

Secretary v. Acchione & Canuso, Inc., 7 O.S.H. Cas. (BNA) 2128 (1980).

Shanoff v. Illinois Department of Human Services, 258 F.3d 696 (7th Cir. 2001).

Shaw v. AutoZone, Inc., 180 F.3d 806, 812–813 (7th Cir. 1999).

Sibley Mem. Hosp. V. Wilson, 488 F.2d 1338 (D.C. Cir. 1973).

Solgado v. CDW Computer Centers, Inc., No. 97 C 1975; WL 60779 (ND Ill. 1998).

Textile Workers v. Darlington Manufacturing Co., 380 U.S 263, 85 S.Ct. 994 (1965).

Torres-Lopez v. May (9th Cir.1997) 111 F.3d 633, 638.

Unger v. Consolidated Foods Corp., 657 F.2d 909, 915 n. 8 (7th Cir.1981), crt. denied, 460 U.S. 1102, 103 S.Ct. 1801, 76 L.Ed.2d 366, and cert. denied, 464 U.S. 1017, 104 S.Ct. 549, 78 L.Ed.2d 723 (1983).

Walters v. Metropolitan Education Enterprises, Inc., 117 S.Ct. 660 (1997).

Whitewood Maintenance Co., 292 NLRB 1159 (1989).

Worker's Adjustment Retraining And Notification Act, 29 U.S.C. §§ 2101–2109 (1988); 20 C.F.R. § 639 (1988); 54 Fed.Reg.16042, 16045 (April 20, 1989).

THE PSYCHOLOGIST-MANAGER JOURNAL, 2005, 8(2), 205–221

Ψ III. RESEARCH TOOLS

Auditing Selection Processes: Application of a Risk Assessment Model

S. Morton McPhail
Jeanneret & Associates, Inc.

A model for auditing in-place selection systems is described. The model is based on a 2-facet analysis that examines both the extent to which use of the procedure is likely to expose the organization to litigation and the extent to which a credible defense of the procedure can be developed based on the validation research supporting it. Several legal, business, and professional issues related to the conduct of such audits are also discussed.

Organizations that have adopted preemployment testing programs to assist in making hiring decisions frequently expend substantial resources of time and dollars in developing and validating these selection processes. Some larger and more complex organizations may amass a sizeable number of testing programs impacting large numbers of applicants for various departments and geographic locations. However, once development is complete and sufficient validity is demonstrated, many organizations fail to continue the research efforts needed to monitor testing implementation and results or to update validity information.

Unless the testing function is monitored, organizations can quickly lose sight of the testing activities, especially if the testing function is decentralized such that organizational sub-units conduct testing at different locations for a number of different jobs. The risk associated with ongoing testing programs is increased or mediated by many factors including (but not limited to): (a) breadth and complexity of the programs, (b) currency of the validity evidence, (c) number of applicants tested at any given time or over time, (d) availability of appropriate documentation, and (e) technical quality of the research supporting the test.

Correspondence should be sent to S. Morton McPhail, Jeanneret & Associates, Inc., 601 Jefferson, Ste. 3900, Houston, Texas 77002. E-mail: smmcphail@jeanneret.com

The process of evaluating tests and testing programs involves a variety of considerations, including costs, effectiveness, and the extent to which testing exposes the organization to litigation risks. Assessment of the risks posed by testing can be complex and is often ignored until the organization is faced with some challenge. To assist organizations in assessing the status of their testing functions, this article describes a comprehensive audit process to examine both the validity and legal defensibility of preemployment selection practices. Many of the issues raised here also apply to other selection processes such as promotions and selection into training programs.

THE RISK ASSESSMENT MODEL

The Risk Assessment Model (see Figure 1) was established to describe and guide the audit process. The model recognizes two broad aspects of risk in the employment litigation context:

1. Exposure: the likelihood that the use of a particular selection procedure will result in litigation
2. Defensibility: an organization's ability successfully to defend the use of a particular test, if it were challenged

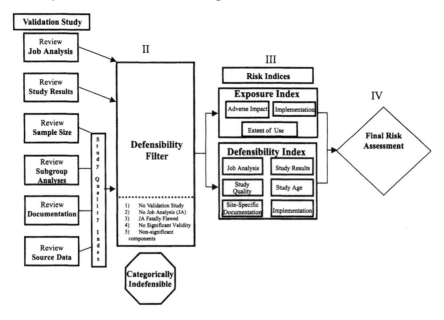

FIGURE 1   Risk Assessment Model. Reprinted with permission from Jeanneret & Associates, Inc. © 1998.

That is, how likely is it that the testing program will face challenge and, if challenged, how likely is it that a credible and effective defense of the program can be offered?

In the Risk Assessment Model these broad categories are operationalized and evaluated by the four components of the model:

1. The Validation Study Review
2. The Defensibility Filter
3. Computation of the Risk Indices
4. The Final Risk Assessment

Each of the four components is discussed below with a rationale for its inclusion and a brief description of its evaluation. It should be noted that the weightings used for each element of the model and the ways in which they are combined are based on the expert judgment of a panel of five experienced and licensed Industrial/Organizational (I/O) psychologists associated with the developers' firm, after extensive review and discussion of the elements. The weights were subsequently reviewed by an additional group of psychologists with the firm and in-house human resources managers. Other schemes for weighting and combining the evaluations are tenable and may fit a particular organization's situation better.

The Validation Study Review

The validation study review involves the detailed examination of a selection procedure's validity research and the associated findings. To investigate the quality of the validation study, data regarding six critical validation study factors are collected and analyzed. A description of each of these factors is contained in Table 1.

A detailed rating process is used to evaluate the validation study in terms of these six factors, resulting in an overall assessment of the quality of the validation study. Each factor is evaluated using a 3-point scale, ranging from 1 (*minimum risk*), 2 (*moderate risk*), and 3 (*high risk*). Specific anchors were developed for each factor at each rating level to facilitate consistency in the evaluations. To the extent possible, the anchors reflect objective elements of each factor that can be observed by reviewing the validation report. For example, the anchors for reviewing the job analysis factor are as shown in Table 2.

A specific weight (ranging from 1.0 to 3.0) is applied to each factor to account for different levels of potential impact to the validity of the test battery. These weights represent the judgment of the experts that the presence, absence, or quality of certain aspects of the validation study impact overall quality more than other aspects. For example, the actual study results (weighting = 3.0) might be considered more critical to the process than quality of the documentation (weight = 1.0). The six factors may be combined into an initial Validation Study Review (iVSR) index, which can be used by organizations with extensive testing programs simply to

TABLE 1
Validation Study Review Factors

Factor	Description of High Quality Study Elements
Job analysis	Job analysis procedures are based on incumbent interviews, questionnaires, and work observations. Important work behaviors are identified and linked to the tests. Criteria reflect important elements of job performance (EEOC, 1978, Section 14.B[2] & C[2]).
Study results	Results indicate significant correlations of substantial size, based on moderate to large sample sizes. Test scores are correlated with important elements of job performance. (Alternatively, evidence of content validity in the form of appropriate item sampling from the job domain has been provided; EEOC, 1978, Section 14.B[5] & C[4]).
Sample size	Sizes of samples used during the validity study are moderate (50–100 cases) to large (over 100 cases; Hunter & Schmidt, 1990; Schmidt, Hunter, & Urry, 1976; Guion, 1998; SIOP, 2003).
Subgroup analyses	Measures were taken to assess and report test fairness and differential validity using appropriate statistical techniques. Potential for adverse impact was estimated and taken into account in the implementation recommendations (EEOC, 1978, Sections 14.B[8] & 15).
Documentation	Sufficient documentation exists, including dates and locations of study(ies), contact names, and means and standard deviations for total sample and subgroups. Full description of the se and application of the test battery is presented, and a discussion of the relevant search for alternatives is included (EEOC, 1978, Section 15.B & C).
Source Data	Source data relating to the validity study are present and accessible (EEOC, 1978, Section 15.B[11]).

TABLE 2
Job Analysis Rating Anchors

Job Analysis
1 = minimal risk
Detailed job analysis based on incumbent or supervisor interviews, questionnaires, or work observations. Important KSAP's identified and linked to tasks and test constructs. Criteria reflect important elements of job performance.
2 = moderate risk
Important work behaviors or criteria not adequately identified. Links between tasks and KSAPs and between KSAPs and tests, not provided. Jobs that appear somewhat different are combined without sufficient evidence or rationale.
3 = high risk
No job analysis conducted. No description of job analysis activities or results provided. Jobs that are clearly different are combined without sufficient evidence or rationale. Multiple job families are identified during the job analysis and then combined without sufficient evidence or rationale.

Note. KSAP = Knowledge, Skills, abilities, and personal characteristics.

compare the relative strengths of the validation research. The weighting scheme used for this index is provided here:

$iVSR = (job\ analysis \times 3.0) + (study\ results \times 3.0) +$
$\qquad (sample\ size \times 1.0) + (subgroup\ analyses \times 2.0) +$
$\qquad (documentation \times 1.0) + (source\ data \times 1.0)$

Four of these factors (sample size, subgroup analyses, documentation, and source data) are combined as a weighted composite (see below) to create a Study Quality Index (SQI), which is used in subsequent components of the model. The remaining two elements (job analysis and study results) are considered so crucial that they have been retained as separate, uncombined entries into subsequent evaluations. The formula for SQI is provided below and reflects the greater importance attached to appropriate subgroup analyses:

$SQI = (sample\ size \times 1.0) + (subgroup\ analyses \times 2.0) +$
$\qquad (documentation \times 1.0) + (source\ data \times 1.0)$

The justification for maintaining the job analysis and study results as separate crucial elements is derived directly from the *Uniform Guidelines*, which state unequivocally, "Any validity study should be based upon a review of information about the job for which the selection procedure is to be used" (Equal Employment Opportunity Commission [EEOC], 1978, Section 14.A). As early as 1982, Thompson and Thompson (1982) concluded, based on their review of court cases to that time, that the first criterion for job analyses used in test validation was "that a job analysis must be performed, and it must be on the exact job for which the selection device is to be used" (p. 872). Kleiman and Faley (1985) reported that in all of the court cases they reviewed, whenever the court undertook to examine the test development procedures, they included a review of the adequacy of the job analysis. The centrality of the job analysis is also reflected in the Society for Industrial and Organizational Psychology (SIOP) *Principles* (2003), which recognize a broader application through use of the term *analysis of work*, defined to "[subsume] information that traditionally has been collected through job analysis methods as well as other information about the work, worker, organization, and work environment" (p. 10).

For criterion related studies, the results obtained (i.e., the validity coefficients) are the *sine qua no*n of the validation effort. The *Uniform Guidelines* specify that the relationship between the selection procedure and relevant criteria should meet the traditional standard of the .05 level of significance (EEOC, 1978, Section 14.B[5]). Kleiman and Faley (1985) indicate that courts have generally followed this standard, though they have sometimes additionally examined both the absolute size of the correlations and their utility in actual use. The *Principles* (SIOP,

2003) offer caution regarding the possibility of Type II errors in local validation studies and recommend reporting effect sizes and confidence intervals in addition to significance information.

The Defensibility Filter

The defensibility filter is designed to identify fatal flaws associated with a validation study that may render the test or test battery indefensible regardless of other considerations. If fatal flaws are identified, support from other elements is not likely to be sufficient to provide a credible defense to a challenge. If one or more of the fatal flaws are identified during the review of the validation study, the tests are classified as "categorically indefensible." Such tests should be immediately addressed by discontinuing their use or correcting the deficiencies. Five factors have been identified as fatal flaws:

1. No extant validation study associated with the test battery could be located (EEOC, 1978, Sections 5.D & 15[3]).
2. No job analysis was reported in the validation study (EEOC, 1978, Section 14.A). (Note that the evaluation anchor for the job analysis factor includes this finding as a component; however, other elements of the job analysis may also result in a 3 rating for the factor.)
3. No statistically significant validity coefficients were reported for the final test battery. (Similarly, the evaluation anchors for the Study Results factor include this result as well as other result elements that may indicate a 3 rating for the factor. It should be noted that there may be situations in which non-significant validity coefficients do not render a test indefensible, EEOC, 1978, Section 14.B[6]. However, a number of other important criteria would have to be met and carefully documented.)
4. Nonsignificant validity coefficients were reported for the recommended tests with no supporting rationale provided for the inclusion of those components in the final battery and with adverse impact associated with those components.

Any selection procedure failing the defensibility filter is assigned a value of 99, which carries over as the Defensibility Index score (discussed later), regardless of the subcomponent scores used to establish the Defensibility Index.

Computation of the Risk Indices

As noted above, two distinct risk indices are used to evaluate the risks associated with use of the selection procedures.

Exposure Index (EI).   The likelihood that an employer will be challenged may be influenced by a great many factors, such as history of past litigation, standing or reputation in the community, and the like. However, three dimensions (see

TABLE 3
Exposure Index Dimensions

Dimension	Description of Exposure Elements
Adverse impact	Applicant flow, pass rates, and selection rates by subgroups. Appropriate probability analyses to assess statistical significance.
Extent of use	Number of locations or jobs using the battery, extent of selection procedure authorization (i.e., how widely has the procedure been authorized for use in the organization, and total number of applicants tested).
Implementation procedures	Existence of standard test administration procedures, accommodations present for Americans with Disabilities Act issues, and appropriate test security procedures (EEOC, 1978, Section 5.E; SIOP, 2003, p. 55ff).

Table 3) explicitly related to testing programs seem most relevant in this context. The first of these dimensions is, of course, the level of disparate impact on some subgroup that is observed in the application of the selection process. This concern is moderated, however, by the extent to which the procedure in question is used. A selection procedure applied to thousands of applicants on a regular basis clearly poses a greater risk, even with relatively low impact, than one that may have higher impact but is administered to a small number of applicants annually. Finally, all other elements being equal, the care and consistency with which the procedures are administered and monitored are important considerations. One must remember that individuals who file complaints or bring lawsuits are almost always people who feel aggrieved, that is, they feel that in some way they have been treated improperly or unfairly. Properly implemented selection systems will provide safeguards that ensure standard administration procedures, appropriate test security, and equitable treatment for all applicants.

Each exposure dimension is evaluated using a 3-point scale, ranging from 1(*minimum risk*), 2 (*moderate risk*), and 3 (*high risk*). A specific weight is applied to each dimension to account for different levels of potential impact on the exposure of the test battery. The EI is calculated using the following formula:

$$EI = (adverse\ impact \times 1.5) + (extent\ of\ use \times 1.0) + (implementation\ procedures \times 1.0)$$

Defensibility Index (DI).   This index is an assessment of the extent to which the available documentation and data would likely be sufficient to provide a strong and credible defense to a challenge resulting from the use of a selection procedure. Two independent dimensions (job analysis and study results) and one combined dimension (Study Quality Index) serve as the first three elements comprising the DI. Other ratings for this index assess the age of the validation study, additional available documentation, and implementation standards.

Of the six elements of the DI shown on Figure 1, three (job analysis, study results, and study quality) come from ratings made previously in Component I, the validation study review. The job analysis evaluation is taken as the rating given during the validation study review. Similarly, the study results evaluation comes also from the validation study review. The Study Quality Index is the weighted sum of ratings for sample size, subgroup analyses, documentation, and source data obtained during the validation study review (see above and Table 1). The other elements of the Defensibility Index are shown in Table 4.

Each dimension is evaluated using a 3-point scale, ranging from 1(*minimum risk*), 2 (*moderate risk*), and 3 (*high risk*). A specific weight is applied to each dimension to account for differences in potential impact on defensibility. The job analysis and study results dimensions are more likely to impact the

TABLE 4
Defensibility Index Elements

Dimension	Description of Low Risk Defensibility Elements
Job analysis (ratings from Validation Study Review)	Job analysis procedures are based on incumbent interviews, questionnaires, or work observations. Important work behaviors are identified and linked to tests. Criteria reflect important elements of job performance.
Study results (ratings from Validation Study Review)	Results indicate significant correlations of substantial size, based on moderate to large sample sizes. Test scores are correlated with important elements of job performance.
Study quality index (ratings from Validation Study Review)	Weighted sum of ratings for sample size, subgroup analyses, documentation, and source data obtained during the Validation Study Review.
Site-specific documentation	Documentation supporting a particular site's use of the selection procedure (e.g., participation in original validity study, transportability study, etc.) for the job(s) to which the procedure has been applied (EEOC, 1978, Section 7.B).
Study age	Recent validity study (within approximately 3 years) or follow-up validation efforts (EEOC, 1978, Section 5.K).
Implementation	Existence of standard administration procedures and the extent to which those procedures are followed over time and across locations (EEOC, 1978, Section 5.E.).

defensibility of a test battery, and thus are weighted more heavily. The DI formula is as follows:

$DI = (job\ analysis \times 3.0) + (study\ results \times 3.0) +$
$(study\ quality\ index \times 1.5) + (site\text{-}specific\ documentation \times 2.0) +$
$(study\ age \times 1) + (implementation \times 1.5)$

The ratings from the validation study review are combined here with the additional defensibility-related dimensions to present an overall index of the likelihood that a particular test battery could withstand challenge.

The Final Risk Assessment

The final risk assessment is based on all factors reviewed during the audit. This final score is used to evaluate the overall risk associated with the selection procedure. The Final Risk Assessment Index is obtained by summing the EI and DIs, as shown in the following:

$Final\ Risk\ Assessment = EI + DI$

Interpreting the indices.   The obtained scale ranges from 21.5 (*lowest risk ratings on every dimension*) to 64.5 (*highest risk ratings on every dimension*), with the exception of those cases which are identified as categorically indefensible, which are assigned a value of 99, outside the normal range. This scale is relative rather than absolute because (as noted above) actual risks in using selection procedures include many factors not considered in this model. However, based on experience in applying the index in evaluating actual selection procedures, the index has been classified into three categories, using the scale shown in Table 5.

These categories are intended for convenience only, and are especially useful for organizations evaluating only one or a few testing procedures. For those organizations which are examining multiple procedures, the index may be used as a means of rank ordering to allow focus on areas needing the greatest attention.

TABLE 5
Risk Assessment Scale

	Final Risk Assessment Score
Minimum risk	21.50–32.00
Moderate risk	32.10–54.00
High risk	> 54.10

SOME LEGAL CONSIDERATIONS

There are two somewhat conflicting schools of thought regarding the advisability of conducting thorough audits of testing programs absent a challenge to them. On the one hand, some researchers (the present author included) have argued that it is better for an employer to know the risks that are being undertaken and where the problems lie so that reasonable planning for improvement and correction of any problems can be initiated. On the other hand, others, including a number of attorneys serving as counsel to employers, take the view that no good deed goes unpunished and are concerned that the employer is potentially documenting a case against its own practices.

Although there are some legitimate protections for employers who engage in self-analysis, many attorneys have found these protections to be less than effective when they find themselves defending a challenged testing program once litigation has been filed. Further, a concern arises that such an analysis may call into question long-standing practices that have been used extensively, thus exposing the employer to risks of class-action litigation or allegations of continuing violations of equal employment laws. Finally, if faced with defending a testing program, legal counsel would certainly wish to rely on the validation evidence offered at the time the tests were developed and implemented, raising a concern that the audit may point out flaws in the research which would undermine their case.

A thorough discussion of all of the relevant issues is beyond the scope of this article but, at the risk of inadequately touching on complex legal topics, the following section briefly addresses three issues that have legal implications as they relate to auditing testing and, incidentally, other human resource programs. The first of these issues is the extent to which the results of such audits can be protected from disclosure during litigation. Second, the business need that may (and often should) underlie the initiation of such an audit is discussed. Finally, the scientific imperative that should impel I/O psychologists and other human resource professionals as scientists and practitioners to recommend and conduct audits and reviews is addressed.

Legal Arguments for Protection

The following discussion provides a very brief overview of some legal protections that may be available to employers if they seek to preserve such confidential materials from disclosure. By way of disclaimer, organizations are advised to seek the advice of qualified legal counsel before undertaking an audit of specific selection systems. Much of the information discussed below is summarized from a particularly helpful review in *The Employee Relations Law Journal* (Hartstein & McCabe, 1993).

Hartstein and McCabe (1993) identify three arguments that can be made to protect the type of analyses described by the risk assessment model: (a) self-critical analysis protection, (b) attorney–client privilege, and (c) attorney work product privilege. The issues surrounding these arguments are legion and complex and have been the subject of much case law in a large variety of venues, most unrelated to employment testing. Indeed, a substantial portion of the case law comes from litigation involving product liability and environmental protection.

Self-critical analysis.   Following a two-pronged legal theory, some courts have held that under certain conditions, employers may not be required to disclose during discovery those analyses undertaken to comply with government requirements to evaluate critically their selection and other personnel programs. The theory argues that (a) employers should not be required to self-incriminate due to a governmental mandate and (b) to require that such analyses be turned over to plaintiffs in litigation would have a chilling effect in obtaining voluntary compliance with government regulations.

There are three important points that should be noted with regard to this exception in discovery. First, legal theorists and the courts place a very high degree of value on the right of both parties in litigation to have full disclosure of the facts. This value is both philosophical and practical. It is philosophical from the perspective that legal theory is predicated on a search for truth that is thwarted by secrecy and confidentiality and on the courts' common viewpoint that there exists an inherent power differential between private plaintiffs and corporate defendants that must be overcome for justice to prevail. It is practical from the perspective that it is the expectation of the legal profession that availability of the facts of a case to both parties will improve the efficiency and effectiveness of the trial process and allow the achievement of the goal of truth to be reached with minimum disruption and costs.

A second point to be noted regarding the issue of self-analysis is that the courts have consistently held that the protection, to the extent that it applies at all, applies only to government required self-analyses (Hartstein & McCabe, 1993). The position is that the government may not use its power to compel a defendant to produce evidence that will be used against it in court. The same protection is not extended to analyses that an employer may undertake independently on its own initiative.

Finally, the protection for self-critical analyses has been further limited to the subjective (critical) components of such analyses and generally does not include the underlying data on which such analyses are based (Hartstein & McCabe, 1993). Thus, the compilation of a database probably cannot be protected using this argument. Moreover, some courts have ruled that not even the quantitative analyses of the database are protected. That is, the subjective evaluative statements that may arise from the relevant analyses may be withheld, but the data and the analyses of the data are in most cases not protected under this argument, whether prepared at the government's demand or not.

A 1978 decision by a district court in Pennsylvania described what the judge referred to as "potential guideposts" for the application of this privilege:

> First, materials protected have generally been those prepared for mandatory governmental reports. Second, only subjective, evaluative materials have been protected; objective data contained in those same reports in no case have been protected. Finally, courts have been sensitive to the need of plaintiffs for such materials, and have denied discovery only where the policy favoring exclusion of the materials clearly outweighed plaintiff's need. (p. 11769; quoting *Webb v. Westinghouse Electric Corporation et al.*, 1978)

Courts in subsequent cases (e.g., *O'Connor et al. v. Chrysler Corporation*, 1980) have cited these guideposts in reaching their own conclusions. Following a period during which the courts seemed to be leaning toward protecting the plaintiff's right to disclosure and full discovery (Hartstein & McCabe, 1993), some cases have suggested a strengthening of the protection in some courts (Felsenthal, 1994). As is true for many legal issues, the matter is not settled.

Attorney–client privilege.   Most people are used to the idea that what one tells his or her attorneys, physicians, priests, ministers, and even psychologists is protected by law from being revealed to others. But even here, in the hallowed realms of such privilege, there are a number of important limitations. The legal theory is based again on the notion that the legal process is specifically designed to seek the truth and that each party in litigation is entitled to effective counsel and representation. The position taken is that one can only expect full revelation of the truth when litigants are free to confide fully in their attorneys in order to obtain appropriate legal advice and counsel. To this end, then, the claim to privilege is generally limited to the communications from a client to counsel for the explicit purpose of obtaining legal advice. Simply having an attorney present when discussing matters related to an audit is not likely to extend the attorney–client privilege to the conversation or to the resulting analyses in most instances. In particular, the courts have distinguished between legal advice and general business advice. Thus, Hartstein and McCabe (1993) distinguish two facets of documents prepared by an organization:

> (1) the communication [must] be made to an attorney acting as an attorney, and not as a business advisor; and (2) the primary purpose of the communication is the securing or providing of legal advice...."[A] document prepared for simultaneous review by legal and non-legal personnel" is not protected. (p. 672; quoting *United States v. International Business Machines*, 66 FRD 631, 1974)

The extent to which a particular court will broadly or narrowly interpret the extension of privilege will depend on the specific facts in the case, the prevailing case law, and the interpretation of the judge.

Attorney work product privilege.   When work is prepared by or at the specific request and under the supervision of an attorney in anticipation of or in response to litigation, the work product generally enjoys protection from discovery. Again, however, this protection is limited by a number of factors. Among these factors are that (a) the anticipation of litigation cannot be vague or unwarranted and (b) the documents cannot be those prepared as a part of the organization's usual business. Thus, the documents cannot be protected based upon a general concern about or an unfounded possibility that litigation might be filed; there must be some basis for the anticipation, and the documents must relate specifically to the litigation and not be something that would have been prepared in any case. Generally, the work product must provide some indication of the attorney's thinking or potential trial strategy that would be compromised by the revelation of the material. Further, material that is simultaneously made available to management or others while also being provided to the attorney would generally not fall under this protection (Hartstein & McCabe, 1993).

Business Management Considerations

Employers generally have reasons beyond legal obligations to conduct thorough reviews of their selection procedures. These reasons are at base the same as those for conducting validation research in the first place. The purpose of validation research is not first and foremost to comply with legal requirements. Rather, such research should be valued to the extent that it provides the employer with a means to determine and ensure that the procedures used do, in fact, accomplish the employer's legitimate goal of identifying and hiring individuals capable of successfully performing the jobs at issue. From the employer's perspective, audits of selection procedures may be thought of as an aspect of continuous improvement that speaks directly to the original purpose for testing, which was to improve the organization's capability to select qualified, productive employees. To the extent that changes in the job or the situation or improvements in measurement technology indicate that other or better selection processes and tools are available, the employer could be making a costly business error not to upgrade its tools and methods, just as it would do on the shop floor or with its computer software.

Moreover, the head-in-the-sand approach may leave undiscovered problems that need to be addressed to forestall even greater problems. Not knowing is not an excuse from a risk management perspective. Unknown risks cannot be mitigated or eliminated. The courts have also recognized this business imperative in considering the issue of protecting self-critical analyses from disclosure and concluded that the need of employers to know and understand their own practices will over-come the chilling effect that has been proposed as a rationale not to require disclo-sure. For example in the case *Hardy et al. v. New York News, Inc.* (1987; also cited in Hartstein & McCabe, 1993), the court offered the following statement as part of its rationale:

> Regardless of whether the News is required to set minority hiring goals, it has an obli-gation to comply with the law and, as a matter of sound business management, has an obligation to take steps to prevent litigation by implementing policies that will im-prove the utilization of minorities.
>
> Accordingly, the failure of the News or any other corporation to initiate and con-tinue aggressive affirmative action programs merely because documents pertaining to their efforts might become available in the context of litigation *would be contrary to basic principles of risk management* [italics added]. (p. 48217; quoting *Hardy et al. v. New York News, Inc.*, 1987)

It is an expected part of the business environment that employers will want and need to evaluate the effectiveness of human resource programs and will engage in appropriate analyses of them on two bases: (a) the need to seek improvement in ex-isting practices and procedures and (b) the need to manage and control risks. Pleading ignorance may be viewed as and indeed probably is, disingenuous or even dereliction of responsibility.

Scientific and Professional Considerations

Both the *Uniform Guidelines* (EEOC, 1978, cf. Sec. 3. B and Sec. 5 K) and the *Principles* (SIOP, 2003, p. 59) require review of validation evidence for currency and continued applicability. The *Uniform Guidelines* contain these admonitions:

> There are no absolutes in the area of determining the currency of a validity study. All circumstances concerning the study, including the validation strategy used, and changes in the relevant labor market and the job should be considered in the determi-nation of when a validity study is outdated. (EEOC, 1978, Sec. 5K)

and

> [T]he use of the test or other procedure may continue until such time as it should rea-sonably be reviewed for currency. Whenever the user is shown an alternative selec-tion procedure with evidence of less adverse impact and substantial evidence of va-lidity for the same job in similar circumstances, the user should investigate it to determine the appropriateness of using or validating it in accord with these guide-lines. (EEOC, 1978, Sec. 3B)

While the *Principles* offer this statement:

> Researchers should develop strategies to anticipate that the validity of inferences for a selection procedure used in a particular situation may change over time....When needed, the research should be brought up to date and reported. (SIOP, 2003, p. 59)

The *Standards* of the American Educational Research Association, American Psychological Association, and National Council on Measurement in Education (1999) include the following:

> Standard 11.16. Test users should verify periodically that their interpretations of test data continue to be appropriate, given any significant changes in their population of test takers, their modes of test administration, and their purposes of testing. (p. 117)

From a scientific perspective, it is clear that, at best, in most situations, researchers are taking a snapshot of a moving train. Jobs and organizations evolve, some more quickly, some more slowly, but they do change. Moreover, much of the validation research conducted suffers from the problems associated with small sample sizes, criterion insufficiency and unreliability, and restrictions in predictor variance, limiting the extent of the inferences that may responsibly be drawn. In addition, psychological science continues to expand with improved methods and instrumentation as well as new conceptual frameworks (witness the changes in knowledge and practice from the 1978 EEOC *Uniform Guidelines* to today). The very nature of the scientific method urges one to question and to reconsider (to "re-search") one's findings and conclusions in search of greater understanding.

CONCLUSIONS

The risk assessment model described in this article provides test users with an organized approach to evaluating their selection practices and procedures. Applied diligently, it can yield early warning of potential problems as well as point the way to incremental improvements in the procedures and the underlying research and documentation that supports them.

Clearly, one of the first steps that a human resource professional should take is to seek involvement and advice from competent legal counsel. It is essential that the issues are understood and that stakeholders become aware of complicating factors such as ongoing or impending litigation, the organization's past history of litigation, and its practice and policies regarding response to challenges. Although in some cases it is true that the conservative nature of the legal profession may place restrictions on the extent and depth of the examination that an organization is allowed to undertake, these restrictions are not necessarily unreasonable. Legal professionals are certainly capable of and willing to understand the issues that human resources professionals bring to the discussion.

It is important to recognize from the beginning that it is extremely likely that such analyses will be scrutinized by opposing counsel should litigation arise. It may be prudent to reserve specific conclusions to presentations rather than a written report, and it is particularly important that the written report not speculate. Sticking to the facts and avoiding projection beyond the data are critical. For example, the analysis may indicate the presence of adverse impact based on the use of a particular test at a specific site. Although such a finding may raise questions about the use of that test elsewhere, one should not assume the existence of such impact without further data and analyses.

Before beginning an audit, it is important that both management and legal counsel understand the potential outcomes. Frequently, the purpose of conducting an audit will be to focus on the bad news. Where are the problems? What is not working? Where do the risks lie?

In some cases, it may be useful and effective to conduct an audit in a phased approach. That is, one may break down the problem into smaller components to define a clear limitation on the findings or to restrict the review to a manageable breadth to allow for appropriate follow-up and action. One might limit the segments of the organization to be studied, leaving to a future date the review of other business segments or departments. The analysis might be limited to only certain jobs, say, those with greatest turnover or greatest need for selection, or only those for which tests are utilized in the selection process.

Under any scenario, it is essential to document carefully the purposes and limitations of such an analysis. One should state the reasonable conclusions that may be drawn from your research before someone else does it for you. If you have evidence that suggests needed changes or improvements, identify them clearly so that the organization can focus its attention on the most relevant aspects of your findings.

Having conducted such an analysis, it is particularly imperative that the employer act on the results. This point should be part of the expectations established with management at the initiation of the assignment. The organization must be committed to investing appropriate resources to act on the results of the audit. Failing to do so may be worse than never having conducted the review. Once the organization has knowledge of the problems needing to be addressed, failure to do so can and will be used against you in a court of law. It is clear that there will arise situations in which it is not feasible to address every problem simultaneously. In these cases, having a clear plan in place for systematically addressing the problems is an appropriate response. You may have to engage in triage to use the available resources most effectively but placing the report on a shelf and continuing on as before should not be an option.

ACKNOWLEDGMENTS

An earlier version of this article was presented in part at the 15th Annual Conference of the Society for Industrial and Organizational Psychology, April 2002, New Orleans, LA. The author gratefully acknowledges the contributions of Darrell D. Hartke, John R. Leonard, Julie A. Caplinger, Mark H. Strong, and Erika L. D'Egidio for their contributions in developing and operationalizing this model.

REFERENCES

American Education Research Association, American Psychological Association, & National Council on Measurement in Education. (1999). *Standards for educational and psychological testing.* Washington, DC: American Psychological Association.

Equal Employment Opportunity Commission, Civil Service Commission, Department of Labor, & Department of Justice. (1978). Uniform guidelines on employee selection procedures. *Federal Register, 43,* 38290–38315.

Felsenthal, E. (1994, August 2). New laws make companies' self-reviews less accessible. *Wall Street Journal,* Section B, p. 2, Column 3.

Guion, R. M. (1998) *Assessment, measurement, and prediction for personnel decisions.* Mahwah, NJ: Lawrence Erlbaum Associates, Inc.

Hardy et al. v. New York News, Inc. 43 EPD 37281 (1987).

Hartstein, B. A., & McCabe, K. A., (1993). Weighing the risks and benefits of voluntary equal employment audits—are they really worth it? *Practical Labor Lawyer: Employee Relations, L. J., 18,* (4) 669—679.

Hunter, J. E., & Schmidt, F. L. (1990*) Methods of meta-analysis: Correcting error and bias in research findings.* Newbury Park, CA: Sage.

Kleiman, L. S., & Faley, R. H. (1985). The implications of professional and legal guidelines for court decisions involving criterion-related validity: A review and analysis. *Personnel Psychology, 38,* 803—833.

O'Connor et al. v. Chrysler Corporation, 22 EPD 30855 (1980).

Schmidt, F. L., Hunter, J. E., & Urry, V. W. (1976) Statistical power in criterion-related validation studies. *Journal of Applied Psychology, 61,* 473–485.

Society for Industrial and Organizational Psychology. (2003). *Principles for the validation and use of personnel selection procedures* (4th ed.). Bowling Green, OH: American Psychological Association.

Thompson, D. E., & Thompson, T. A. (1982). Court standards for job analysis in test validation. *Personnel Psychology, 35,* 865—874.

United States v. International Business Machines, 66 FRD 631 (1974).

Webb v. Westinghouse Electric Corporation et al., 20 EPD 30145 (1978).

THE PSYCHOLOGIST-MANAGER JOURNAL, 2005, 8(2), 223–228

Ψμ IV. SUMMING UP

Forensic Challenges for Managers

Rodney L. Lowman

California School of International Studies
Alliant International University

This article reviews the articles in this special issue edited by Finkelman (2005) on forensic issues important for managers. It begins by contrasting generalist managerial training with the more specialized preparation characteristic of psychologists, suggesting that psychologist–managers have much to learn from technical experts such as attorneys. Common themes in these articles are noted as well as some of the strengths and limitations of the articles in the series. The collection highlights the importance of consistency and documentation, policy development, and anticipation of legal risk. Distinctions are noted between legal and psychological bases for decision making, and several emerging situations are described that may lead to liability and ligitation, such as cell phone and Internet use and employee leasing. Suggestions are made for managers and for empirical research.

This special issue identifies a number of concerns for the psychologist–manager, matters that are often not obvious either to managers or psychologist–managers. Primarily centered on human resources issues in management, this series has as much to say to the non-psychologist manager as to the manager with psychologist credentials. The lead article in this issue by Fodchuk and Sidebotham illustrates how the psychological experience of a violation of procedural justice can lead to the sense of unfairness that can result in litigation.

NEW CONCERNS FOR MANAGERS: UPPING THE ANTE

In terms of content or domain knowledge, psychologists come to the managerial role at a comparative disadvantage from those who set out with a career ambition to manage and supervise others. Psychologists are rarely trained to be managers

Correspondence should be sent to Rodney L. Lowman, PhD, Office of the Provost, Alliant International University, 10455 Pomerado Road, San Diego, CA 92131–1799. E-mail: rlowman@alliant.edu

and it is the unusual psychologist who has gone to graduate school with that career ambition in mind. Still, for a variety of reasons, psychologists may find themselves as managers or leaders of the organizations in which they work. Often this derives from the fact that they are bright and ambitious and good with people so they naturally emerge as candidates when leaders in their particular parts of an organization are sought. Psychologists' mastery of complex material also makes it relatively easy for them to grapple with information that must be considered.

In some senses a manager's job, in contrast to the psychologist's role, is usually that of being a generalist more than a specialist. The MBA degree, the typical point of entry for those who do train to be managers, is a generalist degree. It covers a lot of different aspects of business (accounting, marketing, finance and the like) and then tries to integrate these perspectives together, often through case-study methodology, into a coherent, action-oriented whole. In contrast, the psychologist trains typically in depth in a single area of specialization, capped by very focused dissertation research in a narrow area of specialization. The approach to management calls for knowing a lot (typically in less depth) about a number of areas and relying on specialists when specialized knowledge is needed. In a sense, then, the psychologist must unlearn a perhaps preferred approach to knowledge building and action to become a manager and must often be satisfied with acting on sufficient but far-from-complete knowledge.

Still, there is an ever-expanding technical knowledge base with which managers must be familiar to be successful in their chosen arenas. The technical side of management consists of all of the information, laws, and guidelines that must be followed in executing the managerial role. Clearly, this will in part derive from on-the-job knowledge as one masters the specific parameters of practice in any specific managerial context. But there is also much to be said for expanding the repertoire of one's expertise for situations that perhaps can best be managed by anticipating and preventing the difficulty rather than managing one's way out of a legal thicket.

For example, in my own role as a senior university administrator I spend more of my time than I might have imagined with university attorneys trying to manage legal threats to the institution or extant law suits. The number of cases or potential cases is small in number but the amount of time they consume is large. The issues most typically include personnel matters and threatened or actual legal cases involving students, particularly those whose graduation or continued progress in a program is threatened. I have had to become far more knowledgeable than I ever anticipated in the legal aspects of management and in crafting a preventative strategy to avoid these problems.

TECHNICAL ADVICE

Effective forensic guidance for managers and psychologist–managers consists of both being aware of a litigation threat and acting in a way to minimize its potential damage to an organization. For example, Sidebotham (this issue) identifies a number of areas in employment discrimination in which managers need to be aware of the relevant legal parameters and also of the way the employer has consistently followed its own policies—or not—which will influence how a legal case might go. Both he and McPhail (this issue) note the importance of up-to-date and accurate job analyses (an area highly developed by industrial/organizational psychologists) as the basis for employment actions.

McPhail makes the reasonable case that employers need to examine periodically the preemployment assessment processes they use to consider their legal liabilities to the organization. He identifies a number of important factors that go into determining whether or not a selection methodology is an appropriate and defensible one or one setting up the organization for legal problems.

It would be difficult to argue that the variables included in McPhail's model (e.g., job analysis, empirical support for the predictors used, documentation) are not important ones for employers carefully to review and consider; however, the article may imply greater validity for such risk-assessment tools as the described "Defensibility Index" than may currently technically be justified. No empirical data are presented to suggest that the indices presented by the author have anything more than heuristic value. Because managers (perhaps not psychologists) love to reduce complex constructs to simple indices that constitute a kind of "scorecard," nonpsychologists may be at particular risk for wanting to adopt a system of this type. However, until there is more empirical evidence that such indices have any validated meaning or legal acceptance, employers would be wise to consider the described approach as being at best suggestive. It brings together relevant factors for consideration but does not necessarily reduce them to a single number that by itself would have scale values constituting an appropriate basis for action.

VALUE OF PREVENTION AND SOUND POLICY

Several of these articles point to an important issue regarding preventative work in avoiding later litigation. For example, Glynn and Marshall (this issue) identify how a common situation of "grade inflation" in employee ratings can come back later to cause serious problems when an overrated employee is more accurately and appropriately evaluated at a later date.

Several areas of employment action require special care in processing and prevention is well advised, as well as having a fully thought through and widely publicized policy. Harassment and discrimination complaints, for example, can be expected to be the source of potential litigation and, once made, should be handled with due caution lest they give rise to complaints of improper handling by either the complainant or the complainee. Having, promoting, and acting in accord with the organization's policy on harassment can go far to determining whether such cases are expeditiously and relatively inexpensively addressed or become a threat to the institution itself.

NEW AND EMERGING AREAS

Managers need to stay current with emerging issues if they are to protect and defend their organizations properly. This series of articles identifies several issues about which managers need to become informed, either in general terms or in depth when these areas relate to the practices of a particular employer.

Dinkelacker (this issue), for example, identifies an issue that I suspect many managers—psychologists or not—have not considered. The tort liability of employers for their employees who drive as part of their work (either directly as drivers or indirectly driving their own cars on company business) identifies an important issue particularly as it relates to the ubiquitous use of cell phones by employees. I suspect many readers of this article may be motivated to create or review institutional policies on driving, especially while using cell phones or when under stress. In another article in this issue, Vorobyov similarly identifies the importance of having and communicating clearly defined policies on computer and Internet use, another emerging area of litigation. Employees should know that their e-mail is not private; that it can be used by the organization or litigants against the organization, or by the organization itself in taking action against individual employees. This is clearly important to publicize widely in a well-developed and communicated e-mail policy.

Another new and emerging area concerns employee-leasing arrangements by which employees' services are contracted by one group and leased out to the consumer of those services as described in the article by Song and Turner (this issue). There are a number of complex issues to be addressed when leasing employees vis-à-vis compliance with a number of labor laws. These include the *Fair Labor Standards Act*, the obligation to notify employees in advance of a decision to close a plant, the *Family and Medical Leave Act*, *Age Discrimination in Employment Act* provisions, and Equal Employment Opportunity laws, among others. This too is an area fraught with complications with which managers need to be familiar and possibly to seek outside counsel if needed before entering into such leasing arrangements.

Of course there are many other emerging areas not addressed in this series with which managers increasingly need to be concerned. These include confidentiality of employee data in sensitive matters such as those involving charges of discrimination, laws and human resource (HR) management concerning job sharing, and the applicability of laws from multiple countries' jurisdictions when the employer is international in scope, to name just three areas increasingly important in HR practice. It is difficult to escape the conclusion that today's manager, especially in a company of any size or complexity, faces an ever-escalating domain of knowledge for which content and legal knowledge will be needed.

WHEN LITIGATION ARISES

Most of these authors suggest or imply, consistent with the experience of most who have been involved in actual litigation, that it is better to avoid trials than to find one's company thrust in the middle of defending its assets, good name, and prior institutional behavior in a courtroom. Still, there are times when litigation is inescapable or indeed the wisest or a necessary defensive course of action. Litigation will be facilitated when the company has acted reasonably, fairly, and consistently with legislation, and when there has been good documentation of the facts of the case, as shown by Sidebotham in this issue.

In a previous issue of this journal, Finkelman (2005) provided useful practical guidance on how juries may be influenced in their thinking and behavior. Although his conclusions were more grounded in his considerable experience as an expert witness than in the forensic psychology or decision-making literature, his guidance would appear helpful for those managers who find themselves in the midst of actual litigation. The intended audience for his article appeared to be attorneys but there was much that might be helpful also to managers. Finkelman's concept of the "jury story" assumed implicitly an individual level of analysis: how individual jurors make up their minds. But a jury decision is a collective one and psychology has a lot to say about how groups make decisions; this would have been useful information to have added to these analyses.

Nielsen's article in this issue on the role of HR testimony is also instructive. Although the issues are specific to one state, California often is the bellwether for trends nationally. In effect, HR testimony as expert witness suggests that the field is increasingly being recognized as having a body of knowledge that must be considered by managers in their behavior. The article also demonstrates that legal tactics in cases that do come to trial may center on trying to exclude testimony that an employer might assume would be admissible.

Another article in this collection (Rutter, this issue) raises several important issues about retaliation that confront managers whose employees may have filed litigation against an employer. This advice is well taken but implicitly points to the need to avoid such cases in the first place. The costs in lack of productivity both of the individual directly affected and of the many individuals around that person are far from trivial.

A NOTE ON METHODOLOGICAL APPROACHES: LEGAL VS. PSYCHOLOGICAL

This series of articles is written mostly by attorneys, not by psychologists. Important differences clearly exist in the approach used by each professional discipline to similar issues and concerns. Whereas psychologists look for an objective truth, or strive to understand human decision making in psychological terms, attorneys look to case law as establishing a basis for action. There are also issues about whether psychologists' testimony in court contexts is scientifically accepted by courts or considered to be inadmissible "junk science." Clearly, as a psychologist–reviewer of these articles it is easier for me to identify the strengths and shortcomings of the articles that emphasize psychological themes. The thoroughness and limitations of specific legal aspects of these articles is best judged by a legal expert in employment law.

CONCLUSION

The world of management is increasingly complex. Psychologists who find themselves in managerial roles will increasingly have to become aware of and have at least general knowledge of domains of knowledge that may be new to them. HR issues are especially likely to generate concerns for managers. Mastery of legal matters and obtaining excellent consultation will be important in managing such cases well. Increasingly, cross-disciplinary approaches, such as those involving both managerial and psychological knowledge, will be needed in successfully addressing forensic issues. Prevention is almost always preferable to litigation but when litigation beckons, one's understanding of how juries make decisions and reduce complexity in the face of often complicated knowledge can be a valuable strength for a psychologist–manager.

REFERENCES

Finkelman, J. (2005). Juror perception of employment litigation. *The Psychologist–manager Journal,* 8, 45–54.

THE PSYCHOLOGIST-MANAGER JOURNAL, 2005, 8(2), 229–231

Ψ V. LAST PAGE

The Last Page: Reflections on the Reach (and the Limitations) of the Law

Rosemary Hays-Thomas
Editor

The collection of articles assembled by Special Issue Editor Jay Finkelman for this special issue addresses a wide range of topics in which legal concerns are essential to the knowledge base of the psychologist-manager. When I entered the field of Industrial-Organizational (I-O) psychology, as I recall there was a saying that "Title VII was a full-employment law for I-O psychologists." This idea was based on the results of the *Griggs* (1971) and subsequent decisions and the resulting emphasis on the necessity for validation of tests used to make employment decisions. I-O psychologists by virtue of their training in measurement and in criterion development thought themselves especially well-suited to develop sound selection devices and programs for organizations. The article by McPhail (this issue) reflects that continuing perspective. But there are many other areas, as this issue demonstrates, that should capture the attention of managers and psychologist-managers.

An early and continuing research interest for me has been the topic of pay equity: fair pay based on the nature of the work and job-related qualifications rather than on the demographic characteristics of employees. In studying this topic, I quickly realized that there was a difference between what is "legal" and what seems "fair." It also became clear that the real impact of legislation is only seen after the development of case law; the courts have a critical role in applying the law as written to actual situations as presented in the arguments of lawyers, and despite the so-called "independence" of the judiciary, many political pressures come to

Correspondence should be sent to Rosemary Hays-Thomas, Department of Psychology, The University of West Florida, Pensacola, FL 32514. E-mail: rlowe@uwf.edu

bear on this process. Transitions on the nation's Supreme Court in this summer of 2005 bring this issue into particularly sharp focus.

The articles in this issue illustrate the critical importance of case law. They also highlight the practical impact of state law and lower court decisions upon managerial practice in organizations. Psychologists who practice in areas involving multi-state or even international contexts often focus on legal decisions that impact broadly across state lines, particularly, in the U.S., those of the United States Supreme Court. (For example, see Gutman's articles about interpretations of the Americans with Disabilities Act or the Age Discrimination in Employment Act [2002, 2005].) Textbooks in psychology and management similarly often focus on cases of national significance. But the day-to-day operation of many workplaces is probably more impacted by the provisions and interpretations of local ordinances and state statutes.

In all, this special issue should open the eyes of psychologist-managers to just how complex their jobs can sometimes be. There is an increasing knowledge base in our field and this issue helps us learn more about what we need to know to be effective in our roles as managers.

EVERYTHING IN CONTEXT

The slow, systematic, reasoned approach of the legal system illustrated in this issue stands in sharp contrast to the fast, disorganized, and *ad hoc* unfolding of events surrounding Hurricanes Katrina and Rita during this memorable summer of 2005. And at press time a major earthquake in Pakistan puts even the problems of the Gulf Coast in perspective. These natural disasters and the subsequent public and private sector responses to them have dramatically impacted the lives of individuals, the stability of organizations, and the economies of the affected areas and countries. In the ensuing months and years we will surely see litigation and legislation resulting from these horrific circumstances. Our hearts go out to those impacted by these disasters, who, in the case of the Gulf Coast tragedies, include some members of SPIM and others who produce this Journal. Suddenly, our intense attention to what we know well and do well is entirely upset when our very subsistence needs are at stake. Having lived through and seen too much hurricane-caused destruction of property and displacement of friends and colleagues, I encourage psychologist-managers to seek ways to use their professional and personal resources to ameliorate the suffering that continues to result from these storms, and to build organizations that can better prevent and address such problems in the future.

REFERENCES

Griggs v. Duke Power Co. (1971) 401 US 424.

Gutman, A. (2002). On the legal front: Two January 2002 Supreme Court rulings – *Toyota v. Williams* and *EEOC v. Waffle House. The Industrial-Organizational Psychologist, 39*(4), 58-65.

Gutman, A. (2005). On the legal front: *Smith v. City of Jackson*: Adverse impact in the ADEA – Well sort of. *The Industrial-Organizational Psychologist, 43*(1) 79-87.

www.ingramcontent.com/pod-product-compliance
Ingram Content Group UK Ltd.
Pitfield, Milton Keynes, MK11 3LW, UK
UKHW020428010325
455677UK00029B/1052

9 780805 893854